STRANGERS, LOVERS, FRIENDS

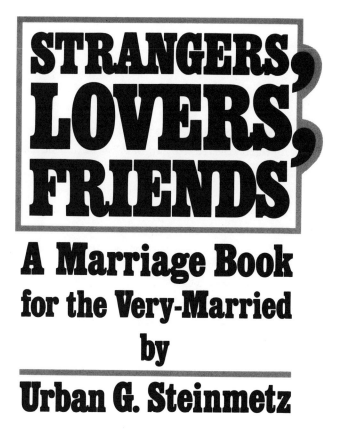

STRANGERS, LOVERS, FRIENDS

A Marriage Book
for the Very-Married
by

Urban G. Steinmetz

Ave Maria Press   Notre Dame, Indiana

International Standard Book Number: 0-87793-217-4

Library of Congress Catalog Card Number: 80-69479

Printed and bound in the United States of America.

Illustrations by Jared D. Lee

Cover and text design by Carol Robak

To Judy, Denny, Jim, Fred, Terry and Debbie, the people who honored us by marrying our children. We want to publicly say thank you for the good things you have brought us, and also say we love you.

Urban Steinmetz
Jeanette Steinmetz

Contents

Introduction

Jeanette and I have a marriage that glows. People tell us that it does, and we often feel it ourselves. We like that feeling, so we try to keep it glowing brighter every day.

So when I was asked to write another book about marriage, I was delighted. It gave me a chance to brag a little about this good thing that we have. Sometimes people need to hear: "We have a marriage that glows. You can too." Sometimes I have to remind myself: "It's real, and it is here, and it is forever. Thank you, God."

Introduction

I wanted to write this marriage book. But when I started to outline the kind of book I usually write, I found myself bored and unwilling. Marriage is not just my life; it is my business, and I've already written a dozen "marriage manuals" of one kind or another. This time the thought hit me—Urb, you're a hypocrite. You no longer believe in marriage manuals. You don't even read them. You do believe that a good and loving God built us all in such a beautifully different way that there is no nice, pat formula for everyone.

And what is the typical marriage manual? Communications, fun and games. I'm OK, you're OK; emphasize the positive. (No one belches at the table in these books. The children don't throw up in their corn flakes.) Parent, child, and adult; how to psychoanalyze your mate. Books by certain trendy experts who have more experience than most of us have; they have been married more times. Experts who spend so much time at seminars that they seldom have problems with their mates. Experts who tell us how to have a swimming marriage—but who never go near the water.

And here and there is a really good marriage book. One that is honest. One that is real. I hope I can write that kind of book. As a matter of fact, I need to write that book.

I need to write it because I am still an

idealist. I still believe that people can treat one another much better than they do now, and that all of us will be happier when they do. I'm selfish, too. I want you to love and be loved. This is a small world, and what you do affects me.

Jeanette and I do have something very good going for us. So good, in fact, that it would take a first-rate salesman to persuade me to trade it for heaven. A good marriage is good for me. But it is good, too, I think, for you. Because I feel loved, cared about, needed, I'm not anywhere near as mean as my early experiences in life could have made me. I'll never start wars. I like myself, so I don't waste a lot of time hating others. I like women, because women have been good to me. But I don't bother other people's wives. Because why bother? There is as much loving in my own back yard as this old man can handle.

Because I am selfish, I want you to feel just as contented, just as loved, just as good about yourself as I do. A happier you is also very good for me. If you know you are loved and loveable, you won't be drunk and kill me while I'm lying helpless on your operating table. You won't rip me off, or lie about me, or beat me down, or sue me, or preach to me. Instead, you will love yourself and respect yourself and accept yourself; and all of this will make life much nicer for me.

13

Introduction

So I am not going to write a how-to-do-it marriage manual. But I am going to write a simple marriage book. What am I going to say? As little as possible.

As I think about you, I am going to be thinking of my children, and the talks we've had about marriage. I'll be thinking about their response when I preached long sermons. I'll be thinking, too, about how excited and interested they became when I said something short and important.

As a matter of fact, you have probably already seen through me. I am an old and tired and lazy and happy former marriage counselor who wants to do something for you, but who knows you will have to do most of it yourself. Twenty-five years ago I knew a hundred thousand important ways to build a marriage, and I needed to tell you about all of them. Today, I remember just a few. There will be no talk about "flowers on her birthday," because some women like flowers, and some are allergic to them, and some would rather have their screen door fixed or the garbage hauled out.

Instead, I will first talk about the real things that happen in every marriage. I hope they help you realize that you are not alone, that all of us do many of the same dumb things as we try to learn how to love that strange and complicated human being we all seem to marry.

14

Then I'll point out some simple directions.
These directions will be neither new nor strange
to you. Jeanette and I have listened at your
keyholes through most of our working lives. We
believe you will find yourselves saying, "Yes, this
is how it is. Yes, it should be this way." We
hope, before you are finished, you will say,
"This is what I want. This is what I need in my
home."

When you make that discovery, the process
of building something beautiful becomes simple.
Give the loving things you want, and that you
need, to your partner.

After a while, you too will have a marriage
that glows.

A Personal Note from the Author (Authors?)

Jeanette and I are confused. We are never quite
sure who writes a marriage book, and whose
name (or names) should appear on the cover.
Our system is this: I do the actual writing, since
that is my "thing." My name goes on the cover,
because Jeanette wants it that way. She does not
feel she can honestly claim to be an "author."

I'm not so sure about that. We spend hours
thinking, talking, even arguing about every
paragraph. If the book is practical, that reflects
Jeanette. She teases me when my writing gets

15

"up in the clouds," and then makes suggestions that bring it back down to earth.

Yet we are both uncomfortable with the "couple" approach to writing a book. That would seem to say, "both Jeanette and Urb are in complete agreement on everything that is written here." That *could* happen after 36 more years of marriage, I suppose, when we are both too old to remember our disagreements.

So if a "we" here and an "I" there confuse you, please keep in mind that we, too, are confused.

—Urban Steinmetz

1

All of Us Marry Strangers

Jeanette and I are sitting in our living room with a young and earnest couple who have just discovered they have "nothing in common." It is harder these days to keep our attention fixed on what they are saying, because this is the thousandth or perhaps the two thousandth couple who have sat before us with nothing in common.

Just five years ago this same couple had "everything going for them." Their relationship was beautiful; they could talk freely and endlessly about almost everything. There were some disagreements, of course, some jealousy, and a lot of fear. But somehow they knew that all of these things would work out in time. They approached their relationship openly, realistically, and a trifle cautiously, knowing full well the horrible statistics on divorce. Many of their friends were already divorced, and both had brothers and sisters whose marriages were shaky. So they decided to give their love a real test before they committed themselves to a permanent relationship. They lived together for a year and a half, and it was good, so finally they said, "This is for life."

And now, they are here in our living room. Neither of them wants a divorce, but they think it may be an answer for both of them. They tell us, "We don't seem to have anything to build a marriage on."

They are talking, of course, to an ancient couple who also had "nothing to build a marriage on." Nothing, that is, that we knew about after five years of marriage. We began some 35 years ago as nearly all couples begin: with "a lot going for us"; with "so much in common." We both liked to play tennnis. We both liked to fish. We both liked to be held. We, too, talked about "everything." We both liked to make love. In those days, it wasn't fashionable to live together, so we started our formal lovemaking by boldly walking up an aisle and publicly announcing, "We will—for life."

Our first year and a half was good, too, because we treated each other carefully. There was something fine in this marriage, and we were smart enough to know it. Sex was exciting, even though it sometimes didn't work too well. Many surprises crept in, but these we did our best to ignore. Our "perfect compatibility" was shaken a little by 20 or 400 differences that appeared, but these, too, we ignored. Both of us knew "my partner will change."

But, by the end of our fifth year, neither one of us had changed. If anything, we had exaggerated our differences by defending them.

I can still remember those terrible scenes in the morning. I am a person who wakes up early, but feeling dull, headachy, and depressed. Since I can't stand myself or my own thoughts, I like to sit and read for a while, while I have several cups of coffee and "come to." The only thing I enjoy at that time of the day is silence, dead silence.

Jeanette, on the other hand, is a friendlier person who can't tolerate long silences, especially in the morning. By 7 a.m., she has endured eight long hours without any conversation at all. To ask her for silence is to ask a bird not to sing.

Our solution was just as obvious 30 years ago as it is now. I get up a little earlier now, have my coffee, and read a book until my self-destructive time is past. Jeanette (who likes to sleep a little longer anyway) stays in bed until the

21

danger is over. But in our early years we insisted on inflicting those fundamental differences on each other. Because she loved me, she worried about a nut who could sit and brood about death, taxes and tooth extractions at such a beautiful time of the day. So she got up with me to "cheer me up."

And I, for my part, demanded that she get up with me. Togetherness, by gosh! I had never had it in my own home. And we were going to have it in this new home—even if it killed the both of us. It didn't go quite that far.

What a bunch of garbage we all learn about marriage! And how impossible it is to build a real, loving relationship until people accept the fact that two real, human, very different people build a marriage in the only way that humans can build anything worthwhile: by trying to discover a path that does not violate or destroy or enslave either one!

We talk to our young couple about the realities that all people encounter in early marriage. They seem encouraged, yet doubtful, because all young couples are alike in still another way. They are tremendously involved in their own relationship and find it hard to believe that other people feel the same things, and with the same intensity.

But what is the basic truth of all marriages? All of us marry strangers; no matter how long we search for a compatible mate; no matter how long we date or talk, or even live together.

We think we marry people who are compatible, because when we are in love we are about as dishonest as people can be. Instead of showing our mates who we are and how we really feel about things, we put on an act; we try to impress; we pretend to be the kind of person we believe our partners want us to be.

We even pretend to be "honest." During our early years together, we claim to talk about "everything." But we don't. Instead, we talk about our little flaws, the ones we shrewdly judge our partners will accept. One of the expressions marriage counselors hear most often is this one, "This isn't the man (woman) I married." Which, of course, is true. The man or woman we finally learn to love, and love to live with, is not the person we married. The one we married was at least a partial fake.

I didn't take long to sense that Jeanette was a practical person. So I talked to her about my great urge to save money and build our little home—even though I have never saved a dollar in my life.

Jeanette likes to travel. So we talked about travel. My idea of a really enjoyable trip was then (and is now) to go across the road and push a boat out in the water and stay there. But that wasn't the kind of trip Jeanette heard about. As we dreamed and planned, we pushed out boats all right, but we launched them in the Bahamas, in Florida and in Hawaii.

Couples deceive each other for many reasons. Almost from birth, we are all taught to "put our best foot forward," to "make a good impression," to pretend to be better (or worse) than we are. When we meet that person we really want to impress, we automatically fall into these old habits.

Then, too, most of us have a poor opinion of ourselves. It is hard to believe that the real "me" is loveable. By the time we marry, we have been criticized too often, cut down too often, been defeated too often. Since we find it so hard to believe that anyone could love the real "me," we try to present a slightly edited and improved version.

Part of the reason that we try to be something that we are not is not dishonest at all. Instead, the "lies" we tell each other may well be expressions of the kind of person we would like to be. By the time I married Jeanette, I was a sarcastic, introverted, quite paranoid individual who had just completed 20 years of constant warfare at home and three years of unhappy encounters with military brass. I know now that I deliberately sought out a person who was outgoing and friendly and genuinely liked people. I desperately needed (and still do need) a person of

that kind who could teach me how to be
friendlier and like people more.

Isn't something like that true of all of us? I
sit in my comfortable living-room chair and listen
to the constant parade of Charlies and Janes who
have "nothing in common." But what I see instead is a small miracle: a matching that must
have been guided by the divine. No person alone
could ever hope to choose his or her mate as
shrewdly as nearly all of us choose ours. We
must have the help of a person far more intelligent and loving than ourselves.

The fact of the matter is this: A marriage
between two compatible people simply doesn't
exist. It can't exist. No one could possibly live
with another who thought like he thought; who
enjoyed all of the same things; who had the same
kind of personality. Such a perfect union would
die of boredom in a month.

Instead, we choose our partners in a much
more practical way. Without even knowing that
we do so, we seek out a person who complements us; who can help us balance the rough
spots in our own personality. That means we
choose a person who is very different from
ourself.

Jeanette and I have had a great deal of fun
with these differences as we traveled from place
to place talking with married couples. We asked
the members of many of our groups to make two

lists. On one piece of paper they listed all the personality traits they had in common. On the second sheet they listed the areas in which they differed. Usually we suggested they take 10 minutes on each list.

Making list one (what we have in common) was always a real sideshow. Everywhere in the room pencils tapped, people stared off into space—intense concentration, start to jot something on paper, stop, hesitate, scratch it out. At the end of the 10-minute period, the average person had three things written on the paper, and often these three had question marks after them. Rarely, a person reached six, and in one case, seven. But just as many had none.

Then we said, "Now list your differences"—and the pencils flew. Many people ran out of paper or ran out of time before they ran out of differences.

These differences come in big and little sizes. Two Catholics marry each other (with their religion "in common") and discover they don't practice the same religion at all. One is deeply involved in the church—with the liturgy, the hymns, the new theologies—and believes almost everything that is said by a priest, a bishop, the pope, or a nun. The other goes to the same church, but is quite uninterested in what happens there. To him or her religion is a process of living, of finding Christ and following him. This person may feel closer to Christ at his or her own dinner table than in the midst of a most solemn service.

Wild spenders marry penny-pinching savers. Extroverts marry introverts. Compulsive talkers select silent types for their mates. Two avid readers join in a "compatible" union—and discover that they do not like to read the same things.

I see all couples I meet faced with tremendous differences, both little and big, and it makes me glad. They may disagree on everything from the kind of toothpaste they use to the time of day to make love. One may be a fighter; the other a peacemaker. One may like two eggs sunny-side up in the morning, while the other can't even stand the thought of eggs. Yet here, in all of these differences, is the only possibility for a real maturing relationship.

I am a self-centered person, who thinks often of himself. Sometimes I wonder what Urb Steinmetz would be like if God had not led him in some mysterious way to Jeanette. I think of the intellectual snob who came out of college trying to snow people with "brilliant" ideas and big words—and the practical high-school graduate who brought me down to earth. I remember her comments on the first things I wrote: "It sounds

27

nice, but I don't know what you are talking about. Don't you want ordinary people to understand what you say?''

I remember this snob who was me deeply and honestly believing what college had subtly taught me: that some kinds of work were more important than others; that ''brain work'' was worth more than working with my hands, so people who worked with their hands were somehow below me.

Just by being herself, Jeanette taught me the pleasure God gives us in simple things, like homemade bread hot out of the oven. By watching her and the different kind of intelligence she showed me as she went about the ''routine'' task of loving me and loving our children, I slowly learned to appreciate and respect the ''uneducated'' people of this world. They are far more ''educated'' and intelligent than I in many important ways. They could fix a car, and I couldn't; they could build a children's playhouse, and I couldn't; they could mend a screen door and fix their own plumbing, and I couldn't.

I have known for many years now why I married that woman. I married her because I loved her, and I loved her because I needed her. I needed someone to help me rid myself of the insanities instilled in me by a home and an education that made me a phony. I had to learn from someone that bodies were just as much a part of a person as souls, and just as important; had to be reminded that doctors and laborers alike pass gas when they eat gassy foods, and that this is OK.

Whether we are ready to admit it or not, God does willingly provide each married person with a mate who can help balance his or her personality. The magic and the mystery and the beauty we see in nearly every marriage is this: We all marry spouses who can help us become better people—if we will let them.

As Christ often told us, one of the great secrets of life is humility. It is looking at ourselves and seeing ourselves as we really are, about half-grown, about half-loving. In marriage God provides each one of us with a mate, also half-grown, half-loving. He gives each one of us a person from a far different home with a far different background and personality to help us complete that missing half. And to make sure that all of this can happen, he provides us with the powerful gifts of sexual attraction and sexual intercourse to keep us interested, excited and involved until we do learn from each other.

Why can't we learn to listen to our partners carefully even before we marry? Why can't we go to the altar with a deep sense of wonder: "Who is this beautiful and wonderfully different person God gave me? How can she help me; how can I help her?"

29

We can't because we have all been so badly trained for loving. Research, as well as experience, tells us that it takes nearly all couples at least 10 years before they can finally relax and say what the French have always said, *"Vive la difference."*

2

The Road to Genuine Love

Honest and Real. In the introduction I promised to keep my marriage book that way. There is a note to myself on my desk that reminds me to say nothing in this book unless I am sure of it, believe it, and have lived through it myself. In the room right next to mine is a woman who will settle for nothing less than honest and real.

About half of this book's readers are women, and I can never hope to cross the gulf between us. Yet all of us, men and women, were very much alike in many of our feelings about ourselves and about our approaching marriage.

Those feelings were far more complicated than we liked to admit.

So let's see if we can continue to describe that real marriage we all seem to live in. But before we do, let's see if we can't first describe both me and you, the kind of persons we were immediately before we walked up that aisle and said, "I do."

We were different, you and I. The part of me that sat and talked with you for long hours was sure of my love for you; sure that I wanted to spend the rest of my life with you; sometimes even sure that I was mature enough and ready for marriage.

But another part of me spent just as many hours alone. That part was not sure of anything. I knew that I needed you and wanted you in some strange and compelling way. Yet I also already knew there were a few things about you that I didn't need and certainly didn't want. Because I wanted the rest of you so much, I tried to gloss over those things. I tried to tell myself that you would change after we were married. But I couldn't make myself completely believe it even then. My mother hadn't changed much over the years, and neither had my dad. Maybe you wouldn't either.

But though I was more uncertain about you than I told you, my biggest problem was still myself. When you asked me if I were ready to marry you, I probably said, "Yes, you know I am!" I wanted to convince you; but again, when I was alone, I had a much harder time convincing myself. Me, ready to form a lifelong relationship with you? I'm not sure.

Love hadn't always worked that well for me. I loved my mom and dad, I guess, and yet there were times when I didn't get along with them at all. Part of the reason I wanted to marry you was to get out of my own home. (I didn't tell you that, of course.) Would I get tired of living with you, too, in a few years? Was I mature enough? Ready to settle down? Ready to assume the responsibilities of a husband? Children? Did I know enough? Was I ready to pay my way in this new home?

Was I mentally ready? Sometimes I worried about myself. So many times I didn't seem to be able to control myself. How would I respond to you? So many times I believed in one way and acted in another—and I didn't know why.

And then there were those fears that we shared during our honest moments. The talks that we had about divorce. Talks that sent chills through both of us because some of our friends were breaking up, some of our closest relatives, some of our immediate families. We visited couples who quarrelled constantly; knew some who abused their kids; were close friends of still others who pickled their love in booze. We didn't dare dwell on any of these. Instead we consoled each other quickly with the thought: "Ours will be different because we can talk about everything"; "Ours will be different because we love each other so much."

"Ours will be different." When I mention that phrase to a group of married couples, chuckles break out all over the room. Men and women look at each other and smile, a little embarrassed that they could have been so naive. Perhaps Adam and Eve told each other that same reassuring tale—just before all hell broke loose.

Certainly young couples are repeating that story today, still trying to make themselves believe it. Not too long ago my son Jim and I were having a man-to-man talk a few weeks before his wedding. Jeanette and I had tried to instill our values in him during his growing-up years, so I felt no need to give him a long-winded lecture. Still, like all parents, I suppose, I knew what was ahead of him, and I wondered if we had taught him enough. So I said to him, "Jim, is there anything you and Terry would like to talk about before your wedding?"

Jim thought for a while, and then he responded, "Well, Dad, I think Terry and I will leave that up to you. If you feel there is something you have to say, that will be fine.

We'll be glad to listen. But frankly, I think you would be wasting your time. We are not going to have any great problems in our marriage, because we get everything out in the open, right now! I know you have seen a lot of marriage problems, and so have we among our friends. But believe me, Dad, ours will be different!"

"Believe me, Dad . . ." Excuse me, Jim; I didn't believe you.

It is true, in a way, that "Ours will be different," because people are different. And yet they are all the same, too, in many ways—in their fears about whether they are ready, in their doubts about whether they are loved enough and loveable enough, even in the certain knowledge that they have been kidding themselves.

Marriages, too, are much alike. The minister and his wife will have a very different style of life than the banker and her husband will, and the factory-worker-couple will live much differently than either of them. And yet, if they are serious about building loving homes, it will take all of them years to achieve a mature and secure love. During that long period of time, they will look for simple answers to love and find none. They will be in love, out of love, feeling unloved, and reach the depths of despair. Many times they will feel lonely and alone because they do not know what is wrong, cannot understand what is happening to them.

What is happening, of course, is the natural process of human love. I don't believe that a book of this kind can shorten this process or make it easier; that can only be done by the couple. All that I can do is describe, as accurately as I can, how a loving marriage develops, so people do know what is happening to them, and know that it is human and natural. The same kinds of things happen to everyone.

All good marriages seem to pass through five stages on their way to mature love, beginning with:

A Dreamworld Stage

This is that first, unreal period of marriage filled with hopes and dreams of a better tomorrow. It is a good and necessary time because we are human, and love is new and we all do need a better tomorrow to believe in.

It is a dreamworld because it hasn't occurred to either one of us yet that our new marriage is like a home with just the foundation poured, standing there open to the wind and rain, waiting for carpenters to come and build it. Somehow, automatically, our dream house is going to get built simply because we love each other so much.

People are touchy and sensitive during the dreamworld stage. At the bottom of that sensitivity is fear: fear that our love isn't strong enough; fears about myself. "If my loved one ever finds out what I am really like, he or she may leave me."

No matter how much we have touched and caressed prior to our marriage, touching, holding, and making love is still exciting. But usually it is not as much fun as we pretend. Deep within us is still another fear: that we won't measure up to the sexual expectations of that other. And, of course, often we don't.

Quarrels during the dreamworld stage are quick, emotional, unexpected—and careful. We are afraid to say what we think and feel, so we make up quickly with nothing settled. It is fun making up, and encouraging, and again we dream: "All of these problems will pass over if we will just give them time. My partner will see the light."

We can be ultrasensitive during this dreamworld stage, so afraid! Outside we are all confidence; inside we are often close to panic. Sometimes the dreamworld seems so beautiful that we move into it and live in it and enjoy every minute of it, pretending to ourselves that tomorrow will never come. And sometimes our hopes seem so shaky that we cling to each other and pray.

As time progresses, the dreamworld fades because it is unreal. Two human individuals have to learn to live with each other and learn how to constantly deepen their love. They have to become friends, best friends, the kind of friends who can confide in each other and trust each other completely. But before any of that can happen, both have to say to their mate, as honestly and completely as they can, "Here is who I am and here is what it is going to take to live with me." Since neither is ready to do that yet, the distance between them slowly increases and their marriage passes into a second stage:

The Time of Disillusion

This is that tough and necessary time we all must pass through if we hope to build mature love and deep friendship. Real marriages are made in this real world, by real people, not up in the clouds in a dream.

At this point, we have lived together for a while. It's not as easy to pretend anymore. That good front we showed each other during the early stages of the dreamworld is wearing thin. We begin to show each other bits and pieces of the real person.

Doubts of love creep in. I still know that I love you (although I am not always sure why), but many times I am not at all sure that you love me—and I cannot bear to stay with you forever if you don't. So I test your love in foolish ways. It's like I said to myself, "I am going to show you the worst side of me, and then, if you still say you love me, I know it will be safe to love you."

One of the ways we test our partner's love is by letting him or her see our most irritating habits. We all bring a few of these into marriage. Some we are not too proud of ourselves; others we cherish. But to our mates, who live right up against us every day, these habits can be utterly disgusting. At first we both try hard to overlook each other's faults, hoping that tomorrow they will go away. But it becomes harder and harder. The relationship is becoming very real. Tension increases daily, and often we snap at each other, and hurt. Nothing changes. Then we shut up and let the hurts build up, and tension increases again.

Sometimes sex is a redeeming thing during the time of disillusion. Sometimes, after an especially good day, we can laugh at those big and little hurts, bury them temporarily and go to bed and enjoy each other. So sex can be good and bad, but often it is bad. We begin to use it as a weapon, a potent way of "straightening my partner out." Someone turns cold. Headaches, sinuses, tired backs, or a "wonderful show on TV" magically appear at sex-time. Husband comes home at 10 o'clock with romantic notions and discovers wife scrubbing the floor and "exhausted." Wife looks forward to a long and beautiful evening—and husband announces that he has a meeting "I simply can't miss." To one of the partners (and this isn't always the husband) sex becomes an obsession. It is on his or her mind almost constantly—and so are the sexual failures. So one pressures an unwilling spouse—which leads to more failures.

During the time of disillusion, both the husband and wife begin to seriously wonder if they have made a mistake. Both daydream (or at least have passing, pleasant thoughts) about other men and women. Since neither one feels sexually fulfilled, jealousy grows stronger. Holding and caressing and endearing words are brushed off or avoided by one or both leading to more frustrations, more failures, more hurt.

Underlying all of these things is a real inability to talk with each other. A dozen serious issues and dozens of minor irritations lie between them needing to be settled. But they do not get into them because both are afraid. Both think, "If we do get into this subject that will be the end," and neither one is ready to consider ending the marriage. Yet anger and frustration and hurt have to be worked off in some way. Almost by mutual agreement, couples quarrel in relatively "safe" areas.

In our own home, the "payday fight" was a regular routine, even though both of us knew it was useless and would settle nothing. We had a family by that time, and there was never enough money to go around. Yet it was a fairly safe way of getting rid of some hostility and tension. It was also sometimes rewarding. Somehow, thoroughly blaming each other for this semimonthly disaster would clear the air for the moment.

But the big issues (and these are different in every home) can't be entirely avoided, either. We live too close. So we pick at these big issues—and then run. Pick-and-run becomes a pattern. I slap my wife with a deeply cutting remark, and she retaliates with something that hurts even more. So then I run: "Oh, there is no use arguing with you. You are always right," and storm out of the house to go console myself at the local pub with a beer. Or she gives me the "silent treatment" for days, and when I finally snap at her, she runs: She goes in the bathroom, locks the door, and cries.

Of course, running away from the real issues causes the tension to increase again. But since neither one of us is willing (or desperate enough?) to thoroughly confront those issues, our marriage passes into a still tougher time:

The Time of Misery

The time of misery differs from the time of disillusion because hope is dead. Neither one believes any longer that "My partner will change," or that "Things will get better tomorrow because we love each other."

The simplest way to describe this time is to say that it is a miserable one. Overwhelming tension is a constant thing; any offhand remark can start a quarrel, or tears, or both. Sex as beauty is dead, or even worse, it is an unwelcome duty. It is here that those ego-destroying conversations take place. In the "depth of passion" someone will ask, "Did you remember to put the cat out, dear?" Or—glancing at the clock—"Can you hurry it up a little? The school bus comes early tomorrow."

There is a change in how we feel about love. During the time of disillusion I thought, "I still think I love you, but I am not sure you love me." But now I think to myself, "There is some feeling for you, but it can't be love. As a matter of fact, I often think I hate you. I don't know why I married you."

One night, when I was describing the time of misery to a group of couples, I used this expression, "During the time of misery, we act like two little kids." Silence in the group. And then,

"You owe all kids everywhere an apology, Urb."
The room exploded in laughter.

Act like little kids? What an insult to kids!
Kids are so much more grown-up than adults are
during the time of misery! Children fight bitterly,
get it out of their systems, and five minutes later
are thoroughly enjoying one another's company.
One small sentence will send us "adults" into a
pout for days. Kids tell each other what they
honestly think and feel, but no one accuses
adults of that same kind of "crime." Children
don't try to change their friends. They are just
happy to be with them.

Now that we are older and the deep hurts
are largely behind us, Jeanette and I occasionally
spend a long and laughing evening watching what
we call our "home movies." We don't "watch"
anything, of course; instead, we just talk about
the hurts and misunderstandings of our own time
of misery. We have a rule for this little game. As
we flash these miserable times across our minds
and our conversations, we pretend we are just an
audience watching two other people go through
this stage. As a result, those "great tragedies" of
our own life turn into very funny comedies.

Those of you who have been married for a
while, can you recall those miserable scenes
without chuckling a little—even though it hurts?
Remember the times you growled to yourself, "If

she really loved me she would know how I feel?"
How would she know, when you never told her
exactly how you feel? Remember the times that
you tried to read each other's minds—and were
dead wrong? Isn't there at least some humor in
this scene (you may have played it for years; we
did): Two people, both wanting to be loved and
held, standing on opposite sides of the room,
saying, "I will love you when you love me. But
you make the first move, because I am the one
who has been hurt the most." But nobody made
the first move, and nothing happened.

The time of misery is indeed a dangerous
time. Couples break up here because both partners keep picking, keep running, and never quite
find the courage to confront each other. Divorces
happen because one suggests it in anger, and the
other is too proud and too hurt to disagree.
Unloving truces are established: "We'll each go
our own way, but stay together for the sake of
the kids." Because some couples are too proud,
or too afraid, or because they don't trust love
enough, they stay in misery, or accept the trauma
of divorce, always to be haunted by the
question, "What if I had . . .?"

And yet, with all of its dangers, the time of
misery is a good, and perhaps even a necessary
time. Humans do not easily change from the
pretenders-at-love we are on our wedding day to
the honest lovers we must become to make a lov-

ing relationship work. It is then that we finally become great lovers as well. We no longer are loving only when it is nice, or when it feels good. We are reaching for that tough love that Christ demands from us: "If you love only those who love you, what merit do you have? Even the pagans do this." Although it may seem that both our marriage and our selves are coming unglued, what is actually happening is that we are finally growing up, finally ready to be married.

The time of misery is not the time to break up a marriage. It is then that we are only inches away from a relationship that glows—even though we seldom or never say "I love you" out loud; even though neither one of us is sure that love exists. Love does exist even on those days that we feel we hate, not love. People don't fall out of love. They only think they do. But their actions prove them wrong.

We have told ourselves countless times, "He (she) doesn't love me," but that is only because we have been so blinded by our own doubts and pride that we have refused to look and see what is actually there. Both husband and wife have said, "I love you, I need you, I want you" in a thousand practical, real ways. We have continued to go to bed at night, even though we knew the bedroom had become a place where we could be hurt and defeated again. We had come home or stayed home on most nights in spite of the terri-

47

ble tension that would greet us at home. We both could think of a hundred places we would rather be. Someone prepared meals—when he or she would have rather prepared poison. Someone provided for this family, even after he or she had come to believe that this home was a lost cause, the poorest investment ever made. In other words, we have shown love most clearly by *staying* there, and by functioning (however badly) as loving people do. "By their fruits you will know them!"

And time has now given us all of the tools we will need to build a lasting love. Both of us now *know* what it is going to take to make this marriage work. We have told each other what it will take a hundred times over— sometimes in stubborn silences, sometimes at the top of our voices, with killing looks, or in some cases, with affairs with other men or women.

So now, after all these years of living together, we are ready to be married. All that is lacking is the will. Someone has to admit: "I must be crazy, but I think I still love you. At least, I don't want it to end." Someone has to turn to prayer and honestly say: "God, I don't know what to do—but you do. Please, help!" That someone has to say, "If I am going to regain his (her) love and respect, I am going to have to make some changes—in me." And at least one person has to start saying, "I guess I still love you; sometimes I think I do love you" until it becomes an honest "I love you" loud enough for the partner to hear. When that happens, the marriage begins to pass into a fourth stage:

The Time of Awakening

This time is very similar to the time of disillusion, but with one big difference. Hope is alive and growing. There are bad days and good days, hurting and being hurt. But now at least one, and sometimes both can see the pot of gold at the end of the rainbow of tough and persistent love.

Hurts have run deep in the time of misery. So there are many false starts before mature love begins to build. There are some plunges back into self-pity and misery because we are too impatient and have waited too long, and we want it all to happen magically, easily, and today.

I can vividly remember one of my own early and fruitless attempts to re-awaken love. I was sitting in the barn, milking the cows, and feeling extremely sorry for me. I was also praying, in my own arrogant way. I told God what a good husband I was, and carefully explained to him the changes that he would want to make—in Jeanette. "Why," I said, "she hasn't told me she loved me in over a year!" Then the thought hit me, "But you haven't told her you loved her either."

Instant answer. Beautiful! Thank you, God. Drop the milk pail, dash to the house, throw my arms around my wife, tell her, "You know, I really love you!" (She will cry, "I love you too, honey," just like they do in the soaps.) Instead she gives me the look that she gives the kids when they dirty their diapers on the way to church. She says, "I know exactly what you love about me!"

End of awakening.

It is not easy to wake up love when it has been in a coma for years. Not easy for your lover to hear, "I am sorry" when he has already heard it a hundred times and nothing ever came of that sorrow. Not real to believe she "will fall into my arms" when you have always let her fall on her face before. Not possible for anyone to quickly believe, "I am loveable; he really does love me," when she has constantly been given an unloving message about herself. The time of awakening is a time for starting over, and this time doing it right.

Awakening is a time of rebuilding. It is patience and persistence and long, long hours of conversation. Sometimes there are quarrels, but quarrels with a difference. We talk them through or shout them through if we must, but we finish them and get them behind us in some way. Some problems we solve; some we compromise; some become less important and disappear.

It is also a time of repentance. Not only do we say, "I am sorry," but we also make some real changes in ourselves. Slowly we discover many things that we can enjoy together and begin to build a real compatibility. Finally we enter that very good time:

The Time of Love

How can we describe this period of a relationship? The one that lasts to the grave and beyond? It is far different, yet much better than anything described in romantic literature. Again, it is real—a deep, human, lasting love that grows each day. A love between two persons who haven't changed that much, who remain different. But we are not just lovers. Now we are friends.

A woman wakes up in the morning and looks at her husband and thinks, "I love you, you big, beautiful hunk of man." And then laughs at herself—because that "beautiful hunk" is short and fat, his morning breath is terrible, and he is snoring. Still chuckling, she steps out of bed and onto his dirty socks, and for one second, the "good old days" come back and she has a terrible urge to stuff them into his open mouth. But then she sighs and puts those socks in the clothes hamper, and thinks, "I would really miss those socks if they weren't there anymore."

It's been a hectic week in this loving home. Saturday night they had curled up together on the davenport, thoroughly enjoying each other, preparing themselves for lovemaking. But just as the wife said, "Old man, I think you've got notions, let's go see what we can make of them," son Pete comes through the door. This is the night he needs to talk. At two o'clock she grins at her tired husband and says, "Oh, well—prepare to defend yourself tomorrow." Five nights and just as many interruptions later he is just as eager to defend himself. Too eager. The lovemaking ends as it is barely beginning. A few years earlier his entire ego would have collapsed with that overstimulated organ. She would have been frustrated, feeling sorry for herself, and believing: "He doesn't care about me! All he thinks about is his own pleasure." But now they both know that tomorrow is another day, and that tonight was nothing more than the sum of a long week, and that it was fun while it lasted. It will be even more fun the following day when they are both relaxed.

So what is the time of love? It is not a time of perfect lovemaking. Instead, it is a time of deeply satisfying loving relationships. It is a time when couples still quarrel, sometimes violently. But no one gets concerned because both know they will be here tomorrow. It is traveling a hundred miles through a blinding snowstorm just to sit with her at your own table. Sometimes it is nagging each other as always, but there is no bite in it anymore. In some homes it is just sitting and being together. This time of love is as different from home to home as people are different.

But two things are always present. The first is a deep, enjoyable friendship and love, which we are careful to show each other every day in ways we both understand. The second is a lack of fear. There is a certain knowledge, now, that our love can handle anything that comes along. To reach love, we have tested it in every way two people can test it. For a time, love staggered and seemed to die or disappear. Yet it was still there.

Mature love has a guidepost, too. It is firmly rooted in an understanding, forgiving, accessible and caring God. It thrives on the certain knowledge that he always wants love to succeed and is always there to help it succeed.

Over the years, Jeanette and I have enjoyed talking about the five stages of marriage. Most people feel good about this description. It lets them know they are normal, and that the things that have happened to them are simply the human things that happen to everyone.

Yet some people are very precise. They can't quite see this nice, neat pattern exactly fitting their own lives.

Of course they can't. The five stages are simply a writer's way of organizing the real things that happen to us as we grope our way toward mature love. Many have told us, "We seem to go through all five stages every day—and then start over the next day!" If you do, good! It's your own special pattern.

The danger lies in hitting a stage and stopping there. Jeanette and I know couples who prolonged the dreamworld for 20 years, and then, when they hit their first crisis, their marriage collapsed. They didn't even know each other. It is easy to avoid confronting the real people we marry when our world is filled with highly developed avoidance techniques. We can greet each other in the evening with a couple of cocktails, which quickly take us away from the world of reality. We can rush out separately after dinner to "do good things in the community." Busybodying other people's problems is an excellent and universally accepted way of avoiding our own. Or, we can take an even easier route. We can bury our minds and personalities in mindless TV, meeting only briefly to "make love" (or something).

Many people hit disillusion, and then get scared. So they make "arrangements": things like the contract marriages we hear so much of today. "You do your thing, and I will do mine, and when we are together, no one rocks the boat. It's too dangerous." Many noted experts hail these arrangements as "the answer," but I believe they can be a disaster, especially where children are involved. Where does a child learn to love when his parents are afraid to try?

Do all couples who stand before a clergyman go through these stages? Unfortunately, no. Too many people make no commitment. They want to get married, but are unwilling to make a permanent investment in marriages. One or the other walks to the altar with this reservation, "I'll see how this goes." And, of course, nothing ever goes unless we make it go. Sadly, these non-marriages scare us all. They are the single largest contributor to our terrible statistics on divorce. When we discount the huge numbers of people who never intended to build a relationship, we may not be doing so badly after all.

But set against this are the increasing numbers of people who seem to have been able to shortcut deep misery and move more quickly toward a maturing love. I think all of us who are parents can help this along. We can tell our children what is ahead of them. They won't believe us, of course; young people seldom do. But when it happens to them, they will recognize it and will be better able to laugh at themselves and move on.

Get Yourself a Loving God

Even among Christians, the gods that we worship come in all shapes and sizes. Often we mistakenly call these gods God and try to use a phony imitation to build a life on.

Much of our Christian world is engaged in the business of telling us about either god or God. Fathers and mothers are usually the first, and they probably teach us what lives with us longest. Politicians tell us about god as election day approaches. More than 200 different varieties of preachers preach god, and sometimes God. Church schools beat us, bribe us, coax us, threaten us, and love us with an almighty.

The trouble with all these gods is that their press agents are people. Usually these people are sincere and honest. But many of them have not been loved enough. Instead, many of them have been hurt too often by too many people. So they cannot see Love clearly.

People who have been punished often in their lives tend to teach us about a punishing god. People who are afraid to come close to a loving and friendly God tell us about a dim and distant one who can only be approached on our knees. People who are insecure give us an insecure god, forever in need of praises, glories and hosannas. Church builders give us a church-building god, while those who worry about budgets present us with a god who first responds to dollars given. From people in high places we get gods who approve of high places and tell us that we must reverence the high office and not the person who fills it. Bookkeeping types give us bookkeeping gods who chart and graph our good deeds and bad, while church organizations frequently offer us a god who is really an obedient second lieutenant, cheerfully endorsing and cosigning any orders that the great commanders of those organizations decree.

Our world, too, offers us a whole variety of gods, although our society doesn't call them that. But when we are asked to devote our entire lives to gathering money or power, to our profession, to education, even to the church, or to marriage, then we are being coerced to follow false gods. Our God is a jealous God, and he wants our lives committed first to him.

The incessant din of all of these gods beats at our head for 20 years or more, and then we marry. Very shortly we discover that no one could possibly live with and continue to love the strange and complicated human being we all seem to marry without the help of that real God who sees things much more clearly than we do.

Unfortunately, that is also when we discover that we have no dependable and loving and real God at all. Instead, four of us enter nearly every Christian marriage: one man and one woman, but both bringing along their own separate and distinct and highly unlikely gods.

Sometimes a couple divorces these useless gods quite early in the marriage. More often, leftovers of these gods hang on, and are themselves the cause of endless, useless bickering. But sometimes—slowly, thoughtfully, prayerfully—God is substituted for these ungodly gods. Then the couple is on its way toward a genuine, mature and beautiful love. Now there are three people in the union totally committed to the same business—the business of creating love. And *one* of these people is mature enough, and wise enough, and caring enough to see through the hurt feelings and the unfeeling relatives and the disgusting habits to the real, loving people underneath.

Because God has been a close, personal and dependable friend for the past 20 years of my life, I have spent a great deal of time trying to tell others about him. Usually I have failed, even with my own children. Now I am facing the reasons for that failure.

God really doesn't need another press agent who loudly shouts, "Follow God the Urb Steinmetz way." Too many people are already shouting, "Here is God," and, "There is God," and confusing all of us. I am sure, now, that my friend doesn't want me to add to the confusion.

The truth of the matter is that each one of us has to find God individually. That is not as hard as it sounds. All that we need to do is sincerely face ourselves and admit that none of us is capable of loving alone. Then we can turn to God in honest confusion and say to him: "God, I am confused. I have heard so many dif- ferent things about you that I don't know who you are or what you want from me. But I do know that I need you."

It may not even be important to know who God is. I do not think it is important to me. What is important is that I know that he is my friend, and that I can go to him any day at any hour of the day and he will listen to me, help me.

I am a person who is often afraid and often confused, and I think you are, too. I can't even imagine going through life without a friend who is never confused and never afraid, and who always loves me. I think it is silly to try to meet and love my wife, or my children, or a neighbor, or any other human being without that friend at my side to advise me.

So how do you find God? I guess I believe now that you don't find God. Instead, you approach him many times a day as a little child approaches his father and mother. You approach him in any way that you are comfortable with and tell him that you need him and that you want to do what he wants you to do and that you want to be his friend.

And then God finds you.

4

Keep Sex in Its Place:
A Very Important Place

Just this morning Jeanette and I went through a daily routine we have followed for most of our 35 years together. I took my shower, stretched out on the bed and waited for her to take her shower and come upstairs. When she came into the bedroom I said to her, "I thought that if I stayed here long enough, someone pretty would come in and hold me."

And five minutes ago Jeanette came in and interrupted my writing and put her arm around me and her body touched mine and she said, "Joy and I are going to town. Do you need anything?'' Those little extra touches keep a marriage from dying of boredom.

Ours almost died during the early years when we briefly forgot how good men and women feel to each other and how important it is that they simply hold one another. Like most people, I think, we got all wrapped up in sexual intercourse in "satisfying" each other and in "proving" our love. Even in such essentially silly things as technique and performance. We somehow overlooked the fact that men and women are almost perfectly designed for love.

Marriage, I believe, is the deepest kind of friendship two people can form in this life. It is deeper than others because it contains a sexual component—a holding, loving, exciting component that helps to bridge the rough gaps in any relationship.

It seems strange to me that many married people almost deliberately ignore that sexual component, and so the excitement slowly dies. When the excitement dies, so does the sheer joy of sexual intercourse—and that is a disaster for any marriage.

For a God who loves us designed men and women for long-term loving. The design is perfect because it is complete. It includes the entire human person, from emotions, to feelings, to thought, to physical reaction. All of these are meshed into the personality, so that one man and one woman can form an enduring, maturing relationship.

Enduring, maturing relationship—that is what a loving life is all about. The fun and games of sexual intercourse are fine for the short run; almost anyone can enjoy them. A man or woman can purchase books, study them and become expert. If couples have sexual hang-ups, they can go to a Masters and Johnson-type clinic and get rid of them. Or they can practice a lot, with many partners, and quickly learn all that there is to know about the sex act.

Sexual intercourse is not that complicated. People have been performing it with at least some degree of competence for thousands of years. It frightens me to know that many people in our society make a very good living teaching sexual intercourse, and some even devote their entire lives to this "cause." Yet everything I have learned about its pleasurable performance can be stated in this brief paragraph:

In a satisfying act of sexual intercourse, a rigid (or even semisoft) penis is inserted into a vagina that is soft and pliable and lubricated. To prepare for this insertion, the man and woman stimulate each other in any and all ways that bring them *mutual* enjoyment and sexual excitement. Once the act is begun, the couple continues that act until *both* feel relaxed and contented.

And here, in the two words I have empha-
sized above, is the key to sexual intercourse.
Mutual enjoyment, continued until *both* are
relaxed and satisfied—these brief phrases explain
nearly all of the sexual happiness and unhap-
piness we have seen in more than a quarter of a
century of working with marriage. They explain
why casual encounters with near strangers often
seem beautiful, while married intercourse is frequently a disaster. They explain why adulterous
relationships sometimes feel "right" and
"good," while the same act, performed by a
legally married couple, often leaves the woman
feeling used and the man a failure.

Mutual enjoyment. That is what sexual intercourse is. That is why our friend God designed
this all-absorbing entertainment: to smooth over
the rough days and make the good ones better.

I sometimes wonder what sex would be like
if the whole process of "civilization" were
reversed, and all of those unrealistic teachings
about sex—and all the teachers—were completely
eliminated. I would start in the Garden of Eden
with the devil, and blip him out before he could
tell Eve that her nakedness was shameful. I'd
suggest St. Augustine and the like go to an early
and well-earned reward—before they could tell us
about women as temptresses and the horrible
consequences of even thinking about "that sin."
I'd move down through the centuries and

discover all preachers of both sexes and many oc-
cupations, and catch them just before they first
wrote the words ADULTERY and FORNICA-
TION in glowing white chalk on the big, black
blackboards of uncounted innocent minds.

Finally, I'd arrive at our present day and
here really get busy. I would take Hugh Hefner
and all of his bunnies and all of his imitators to
a desert island—with no communications from
that island—and leave them to fantasize in peace.
All of the writers who so vividly describe the 76
different sexual positions (including swinging
from the shower bar) could be packed away in
abandoned monasteries where they could titillate
one another with their dreams of sexual prowess.
And all of the so-called "experts on human sexuality" would be tapped on their shoulders
before they left for their lectures and workshops
and seminars—and reminded that they have people at home who need loving. If somehow all
references to sex in all of our histories could be
eliminated what would finally be left would be
people.

Sexual people. Beautifully designed by their
friend God for loving. Designed with all of their
sexual emotions and feelings in place, ready to be
used as love unfolds.

Such people wouldn't know that little boys
don't associate with little girls, because no one
would have told them. They could play together,

study together, talk honestly with one another, and come to understand and know one another very well. They would also come to know and respect the real differences between them.

I wonder how much "knowledge" these people would need when they finally selected their lifelong mates. It seems to me that our friend God wanted us to enjoy sexual intercourse, or he wouldn't have designed our bodies and minds in the way that he did.

When a man is attracted to a woman, he wants to be with her, to talk to her, to hold her—naturally. As his feeling of attraction deepens, his blood pressure increases, his breathing quickens, his penis erects—naturally. He throws no switches; he makes no decision to place his emotions on "go." Instead, all of these things happen to him because he was designed that way.

When a woman is attracted to a man, she, too, wants to be with him, wants to talk to him, wants to hold him or be held by him. As her attraction deepens, her body, too, begins to prepare itself for intercourse. Her pulse and blood pressure increase, her breathing quickens, the tips of her breasts become firmer, the clitoris erects and becomes sensitive, and the vagina begins to lubricate itself.

These feelings are common to everyone. Someone created these feelings. Someone who loved us wanted to make it simple for a man to love a woman; for a woman to love a man. Someone wanted us to learn to feel deeply and completely, so that it would be much easier to experience love and in that process learn to love God, our neighbors, our children and our friends. Someone had confidence in us when he gave us this great gift. He gave us feelings so beautiful and so absorbing that it would be foolish to want to destroy them.

We are children of God, persons of immense dignity. We are sons and daughters of our Father, and because love is his business, it is our business. We all want to love and be loved. We all want to hold and be held. Men and women want, and perhaps need, the feeling of total love that comes through total union. Neither a man nor a woman would deliberately destroy this great beauty and sheer pleasure.

Yet, like fools, we do destroy it in great numbers, daily. Jeanette and I destroyed it for ourselves for a long time. Looking back on it, neither one of us can feel guilty. We know that neither one of us set out to deliberately hurt the other sexually. I know that I never wanted to make her cold and unresponsive. She knows that she did not deliberately rob me of my sexual confidence and even ability. And yet, that is what we succeeded in doing to each other.

We did it for two reasons. The first was

because we loved each other very much (although we didn't know it or wouldn't admit it at that time). No one else could hurt me the way Jeanette could hurt me; no one else could hurt Jeanette the way I could hurt her. So how we treated each other was of overwhelming importance. We became so careful of each other we were not honest. As I said earlier, lovers are liars.

But the second reason can best be described in Jeanette's own words, "We were stupid, honey, just plain stupid." She uses that expression often when we carefully talk about those bad old days. "Stupid" is a rough word, yet it is also a forgiving one. I can see my God severely condemning us for deliberately destroying love. But I can't see him being anything but understanding of honest stupidity.

We were stupid because we believed the things our world had taught us about sex. Believed might not be the proper word; absorbed might be more accurate. I am not sure I ever believed that the man must be the undisputed "head of the household," and yet that's the way I acted. I don't think I ever fully believed that sex was a wife's "sacred marital duty" and yet I can remember repeating it, hurting Jeanette with it, hurting me with it—because that stupid idea was, somehow, an absorbed part of me.

And then there was the "information" I had

absorbed in bars, in barracks, in dormitories and in all-male "bull sessions." Information that put all women in one slot, as people who wanted to be conquered and taken. Boastful, insecure lies repeated so often that they became perverted truths and mixed-up convictions. All of women's problems could be solved with a "good roll in the hay."

How stupid all of this misinformation becomes when we are faced with continuing, long-term sexual relations between real people. Male psychologists peer over their ritualistic beards as they "diagnose" and "treat" severe impotency problems. Yet some "impotency problems" are the result of feeling like a failure—and we all feel like failures now and then. Sexologists earnestly gather "accurate statistics" and publish these statistics as "facts." People buy these misrepresentations and then try to impose them on already angry mates. Physicians pack the sexually frustrated into their offices in droves. Some physicians can help, but most can only show us what our organs are and how these organs operate. Pornographers, whose only intention is to make a buck, suddenly find themselves overwhelmed with purchasers so desperate they will turn anywhere for advice.

Only the married couple can solve a sexual problem. One hour of good conversation in a bedroom is better than 100 hours on a psychiatrist's couch. One ounce of humility is worth more than one ton of "sex education." There is nothing in the whole realm of sexual expertise so effective as these three little sentences: "Honey, I really want to love you, and I want to make you feel loved. But I don't know how. Can you help me?"

All of us (and there are a great many of us) who have achieved a loving sexual life have come to realize that lasting satisfaction is not a process of education. Instead, it is a process of unlearning, and then relearning.

All of us bring two things to bed with us when we marry:

1. The things we have learned about sex since birth, and

2. The beautiful things that we sexually are.

And, in all cases in today's world, much of what we have learned about sex since birth is garbage.

It is true that some parents today are very much in love with each other, and so they do an excellent job of showing their children the possibilities of a loving sexual life. It is equally true that some few sex educators are themselves very comfortable sexually, and so are able to impart a comforting view of human sexuality to their students. But it is never true that any one individual arrives at marriage sexually mature.

It is impossible to arrive at marriage sexually

mature because all of the people of our world are engaged in "sex education." The English teacher who always has a sarcastic comment about men is teaching sex education. The businessman who pursues his own private bunny club is engaged in sex education. Gynecologists who remove ovaries like busy squirrels storing hickory nuts are saying something to us about sex. Soap operas number their students in the tens of millions.

In a world obsessed by sex we receive much more misinformation that we do information. In our own little world of friends and relatives, we usually are close to many who are divorced or at least unhappy in their marriages, and to few who are happy. If we turn to professionals of any kind for advice, the odds are better than good that we are asking the blind to help us see. Books are a real jungle, with a tiny proportion written responsibly and the vast majority produced because sex sells.

So the things we have learned about sex are largely garbage, garbage we must discard before we can hope to live mature and loving lives.

Jeanette and I have already spent thousands of hours "cleaning out the garbage" from our own sexual lives, and it is a process that will never be finished. In today's mass-communication world, brand-new garbage comes in almost as fast as we can shovel it out.

Our main cleaning tool is conversation. We

try to explain to each other who we are and what we were taught and why we feel as we do. It is a healing process, too. As I tell her about college and its emphasis on masculine "rights" and feminine "duties," both she and I realize that, in the early years of our marriage, I was only acting "right" as I was taught to act. Slowly we have learned that we are not "bad people," but we have been badly taught.

That knowledge gives us the confidence we need to try to discover the beautiful things we sexually are. All of us are born children of God, and so we are persons of immense dignity. We are beautifully designed for loving. That friend who loves us helps us choose a mate who complements us, who can help complete us. And he stands with us every step of the way as we try to mature in love.

His constant companionship has helped us to realize that there are few, if any, sins in the bedroom. What increases our love for each other increases our love for him.

But there is a lot of stupidity in everyone's bedroom, including our own. In fact, there are stupidities all through our homes, and all through our married lives. It is stupid to treat a person like a dog all day long, and then expect him or her to "turn on" at bedtime. It is stupid to think that a child of God can be ignored at all hours, and then loved at a magic hour.

It is nonsensical to put a stopwatch on intercourse, and stop it when *one* of the parties has an orgasm. In lovemaking, what happens to organs is not important; what happens to people is. No one keeps score in the depths of passion.

There is an old-fashioned expression that goes like this: "Love is the cake, and intercourse is the frosting on the cake." In temporary encounters or short-term, live-in situations that may not always be true. In these intercourse sometimes *is* the cake, because it is the only thing either one is thinking about. When the whole person is not completely involved, bodies can be manipulated, stimulated, excited and satisfied.

But in the intense relationship of marriage, people have committed themselves to something much deeper and better. Here, intercourse is the "frosting on the cake," and it won't frost right unless the cake is baked with care.

In this long-term relationship, the primary sex organ in both the man and woman is located squarely behind the eyes. The brain rules the body, and tells it what to do. If a mind feels loved, cared about, important, needed, it functions in a beautiful way. But a mind that feels depressed, unloved, ignored, put down and unimportant often will not function at all.

And these are sexual minds: a woman's mind designed to want a man, and a man's to want a woman. It takes a great deal of time and

patience to remove the scars of fear and misinformation, poor training for love. Perhaps they
never can be completely removed. But the
rewards for following and building on the basic
design of our friend God are very great. To help
a woman feel like a queen, to help a man feel
like a king is the most loving thing a person can
do.

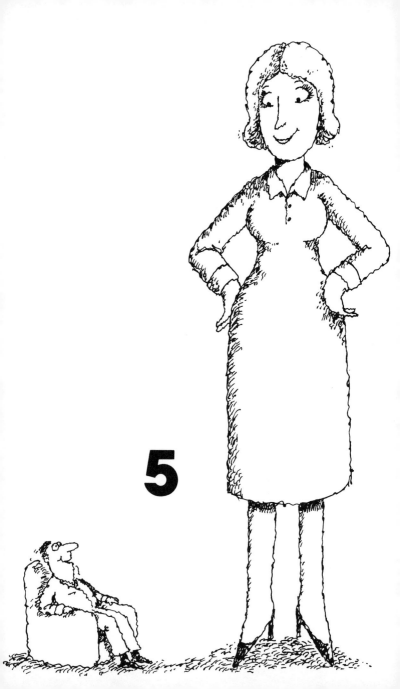

5

Building You
Is Good for Me

Marriage has a certain simple, selfish logic. It is crystal-clear in every relationship, and it goes like this:

Building you is *very good*—for *me*. When I make you feel loved, and important, and good about yourself, you are a dream to live with. Putting you down is *very bad*—for *me*. When you feel unloved, unimportant, and unsure of yourself, you are a miserable person to live with.

The crazy, mixed-up, reverse logic of love! Love doesn't work the way everything else works. That is why it takes most of us so long to try it. In our world, if I own a little car and give it away, I don't have a car anymore. Yet if I own a little love, and I give it all away, I somehow wind up with much more love for myself.

Love is the miracle of the loaves and fishes all over again. You remember the story: Christ had a few loaves and a couple of fish, and 5000 people to feed. He told his apostles to pass out those loaves and fishes, and they did. When they had finished feeding everyone, they collected what was left over and had much more than when they started.

That same miracle is freely given to all of us who marry. At the time of our wedding, you and I are like two loving cups about half full of the things we need to build a loving relationship. Love is strong, but there are those doubts. Trust? Yes, we trust ourselves and trust each other—but not very far. Maturity? I am mature, but you haven't quite arrived (and I am not that sure about me). Do we know how to build this dream marriage? Well, sort of; the details will take care of themselves.

Two loving cups, both about half full. Two people who hope that marriage will fill them and complete them. But two people who do not understand that certain, simple logic of love:

1. If we treat each other very carefully, both trying to hang onto what little love we have in our cups, that love will finally, slowly evaporate.

2. If we try to rob our mates and take what is in them without giving much in return, those fragile cups will finally crack from the rough handling. We will find ourselves living with empty people who have nothing to give.

3. But at any time in our relationship, either one of us can stop that slow seepage and seal those cracks. When we decide to pour all that is good in us into each other, we will both feel better about ourselves.

4. If I continue to pour my own increasing love, self-confidence and respect into your cup, it will finally overflow. And because I am the person who helped you feel loved and complete, those warm and good things that I gave you will overflow—on me.

Unfortunately, we are "trained" for love by a variety of people who know little about love. We don't give things away in this world of ours; we try to accumulate more. We seldom think of love as *building another,* or of *filling* or *completing* another. Instead we think about love as something that "happens"; something that "comes to me."

And love did "happen," did "come to me" in the period before we married. It happened because our sexual attraction was strong, and we wanted to make it stronger. It happened because we did build each other at that time, did give our partners the things they needed to make them feel full and complete.

But then, in the reality of 24-hour living, we all seem to return to our same old conditioned selves. We size up our marriage, and size up our mates, and decide that we don't want them quite like they are. Some changes will have to be made, not in me, but in you. We decide to "help" our partners "mature" (and mature means, of course, "think and act in a mature way—like I do").

Jeanette still remembers the first help I offered her, "Honey, that isn't a piece of cardboard you are frying; it's a steak."

And I remember her helping me: "Is that all you think about? Can't you just hold me once in a while, like you used to?"

When I am in love, and am still unsure of my partner's love, being helped hurts. It says to me, "She doesn't like me the way I am." The surprising thing about those early days of marriage is that no one intends to hurt. In that "clear," worldly logic of ours, our thoughts go something like this: "I thought that I married a certain kind of person. But he (she) isn't the person I thought I married. So I am going to have to help him (her) change."

Now we have two hurt people, neither one of whom feels whole and complete. Both are still very much in love; both are saying to themselves,

"You could be a perfect mate if only you would
. . ." and then they set about the chore of
changing each other in earnest.

Those of you who have been married for a
while know all about changing your partner. It is
a real loser's game. You have tried to help your
partner see the "right" way of doing things for
years, but no one actually changes another
through suggestions, or through pressure, or even
through force. If you apply enough pressure,
your partner may seem to change and agree with
your point of view. But those changes are super-
ficial. People change only when they want to
change, and are ready to. Real changes occur only when the person feels loved.

Still, we persist in trying to change that
other, perhaps because we have to. That person
has one idea of what this relationship should be,
and I have another. We can't both be right—and
if I admit that she is right, then that means I am
wrong. I am going to have to prove to her that I
am right—by proving she is wrong.

But when I tell her she is wrong, I am hurting her, cutting her down, taking a little of that
confidence and self-esteem out of her cup.

And what a fool's game we start here! There
is another strange thing about love: Nobody puts
down a child of God and gets away with it. As
sons and daughters of the Most High, we are all
created in immense dignity. When I try to put

her down, it is beneath her dignity to stay down. She is going to try to get up again—even if it means stepping on me.

So she does try to get up again—and puts me down in the process. Now we are in that terrible trap: I hurt her, and then she hurts me.

And since I *do* love her, what she says and does is important to me. I do want to please her. When she strikes out at me, she makes me feel like a failure—so I let her know she is failing me.

Finally we are both so blinded by hurt and feel so down that we turn vicious. Now all I want to do is hurt her as I have been hurt. We go for the jugular. We even attack each other's basic masculinity and femininity. Any weakness is fair game:

"I thought I married a man." "You're as frigid as your old lady." "My mother was right; you are an animal." "You're a real slob." "I wish I'd married—."

Unfortunate, sometimes disastrous, but true. When Jeanette and I were preparing to write this chapter, we spent a long evening discussing it because we were determined to try to stick to our two goals for this book: honest and real. We were sure of our facts. We did our homework. All loving couples do get into this cutting-down trap sometime during their married lives.

There is no set pattern to hurting, of course. We use the weapons we are familiar with. Some of us attack our mates with sarcasm; some with violent and exaggerated anger; some with sweetness; some with martyrdom; some with silence. Some of us crucify our mates in public; others try to use our children as weapons; still others confine our viciousness to the privacy of our own homes. We hurt each other by secrecy, distrust, jealousy. We hurt each other by running away, by being deliberately inconsiderate, by drunkenness. We hurt each other with outrageous purchases, sometimes even by liaisons with other men or women. We all have our own unique weapons, but all of them are sharp because our beginning love is strong.

We knew when we began this book that this would be our toughest chapter, because all of this hurting and hurting back is so senseless, so destructive. Yet we both feel that the trap is unavoidable. We are all immature when we marry. Love is strong, so hurts do go deep. Human beings are good. They will not let another continue to step on them. They will fight back in some way.

Right at this point in our discussion, Jeanette made a little speech. She felt it was our job to tell people about this trap, so that when young marrieds found themselves sliding into it, they could do something about it quickly. The bottom of that trap is too tough, she felt. Those who escape through divorce are bruised and battered and beaten. Even those of us who hit that bottom and then rebuild carry scars for a long, long time. The old expression that we do forgive but it is hard to forget is certainly true.

We both agree that there are no villains in this trap. Few of us understand what we are supposed to be doing in marriage, because we haven't been prepared. We can't blame our lack of instruction on our parents and teachers, because few of them have really understood what marriage is all about. They, too, groped and fought and hurt just as we have done. And too few finally discovered that it is better to build than to try to dominate, change and destroy.

Simply stated, *the purpose of marriage is the continuing creation of loving people.* It is the only explanation that fits the facts of marriage as we see them, and as you can see them in your own lives. Since two strangers do come into marriage unfulfilled, immature and incomplete, the only possible answer is to build one another. Disaster results from anything less.

I use the words "continuing creation" (of loving people) deliberately because I think God actually assigns husbands and wives the task of completing the job he so beautifully began.

I believe it because I have been able to see that creation at work in our own lives and in the lives of a great number of our friends over a long span of years. It is beautiful to watch what happens to people who know they are loved. Their personalities expand almost unbelievably. Talents that they never knew they possessed continue to appear. Each passing month brings a new and better person, another exciting discovery.

All of this brings pride in the giver of love, too. Pride in the fact that I have had a hand in that flowering. I am proud of Jeanette. She is not the person I married. She is a much better and greater and bigger one. And as arrogant as this may sound, I am not the person Jeanette married. In many ways I, too, am better and bigger and greater. All of this happened because we discovered the miracle of love, the miracle of building one another.

But we are not as great as we were *designed* to be. There are too many hurting, destructive years behind us. We both inflicted too many wounds that still throb on rainy days. We do have a marriage that glows, but we often wonder what it could have been if we hadn't shed so much of each other's blood.

And this, I think, is what we want to say as we move on to the process of building love. Perhaps that cutting-down trap is unavoidable. It seems to be, since all couples who finally reach a maturing love fall into it. Perhaps it is even necessary, because through those hurts we do reach a certain humility, a knowledge that we can never learn to fully love another strange and complicated human being without the help of that Someone who can see love clearly. It is in the depths of failure and despair that we often realize that we must discover the will of that Someone, and follow that will instead of our own.

6

Throw Out All the Rules—
Except Two

Usually I don't like to preach to anyone, because I don't like people to preach to me. Yet as I start this chapter, I feel a great urge to grab hold of my readers and say: "It is all so clear! All so simple! There is a pattern of loving that has worked for the few who have tried it for nearly 2000 years. Why stumble around looking for guidance from human experts, when guidance from God is here in front of us, and it works?"

But why preach? Preaching doesn't help, and I know it. I listen to the great evangelists of our time filling the airwaves with the sound of God, and I see people marching to the front to be saved by the thousands. Yet there doesn't seem to be much more love in our world than there has ever been.

Sometimes I think that our great preachers make so much noise about so many things that they confuse us all. They want us to know every word and all of the meanings of those words in a bible that is huge, and all of this to convey a message of love that is so simple that any child can understand it.

Christ was more efficient. He spent his entire life talking about just one subject, and living it. That subject was love. To make sure that we didn't get confused, he summarized his entire teaching in two short statements:

> You must love the Lord your God with all of your heart, with all of your soul, and with all of your mind. This is the greatest and the first commandment. The second resembles it: You must love your neighbor as yourself. *On these two commandments hang the Whole Law, and the Prophets also.*

So this is what we are to concentrate on to be happy in life and in marriage. Love God; love ourselves; love one another.

But how do we go about building this love? His second short summary explains: "So always treat others as you would like them to treat you; that is the meaning of the Law and the Prophets."

Now it is clear to me why Christ said that "the whole law, and the prophets also" are summarized in these two short paragraphs. I know that if I live by those two rules I will be a happy man. When I give love and feel loved I have everything. And when I treat all others as I want them to treat me, I do give love, and I know I am loved by many in return.

When I married Jeanette the pattern of life was not that clear. Christ's two summaries were just two short paragraphs in a whole big book and in an even bigger church. Those paragraphs were swallowed in the immensity of it all. Standing alongside the church and the bible were thousands of so-called experts on marriage with millions of words and thousands of rules and suggestions for loving. Is it any wonder that we all get confused? That we waste so many valuable years hurting ourselves and each other before we discover what marriage is all about?

End of Sermon. The "gospel" of marriage according to Urb Steinmetz is a simple one. Memorize Christ's two summaries. Think about them. Live them and you will be happy

"Great sermon, Urb." "Thank you, Urb."

But meanwhile, back in the home, how does all of this work out in real life?

First of all, there is that thing about "loving God, with your whole mind, heart and soul." What does that do to the love between a man and a woman? Put God first in your affection? Jeanette doesn't even like it if I pay too much attention to professional football. How is she going to feel about having God for competition?

The answer that strikes me is that God is not competition. Instead, in a very real sense, God is me; God is what I am all about. What I feel about him largely determines how I feel about myself. God is all of the things that are good about me. He is integrity and he is dignity: he is love and he is happiness. And, perhaps most of all, he is understanding and acceptance.

If Jeanette and I try to build a love alone, depending entirely on ourselves, there is nothing we can do but fail. How does a man understand a woman who can bury her head in a broken TV set, completely forgetting that she has a husband, or children until that TV is fixed? How does a lazy man accept a wife who is a workaholic, a woman who must be busy all of the time, who sometimes even wakes up tired from working in her sleep?

How does a woman accept a man who likes to play at carpentry, but who never gets anything square? Believe a man who tells her five times a day, "I'll get it for you, honey," and then promptly forgets what he went after? Simple things. Everyday things. How do any of us understand and accept lovers who grind their teeth in their sleep, pick their noses, drop ashes on the floor, talk too much, and paint their living rooms outrageous colors? In other words, how do people ever succeed in living with people?

The answer has to be, love God first. Then love for that other will fall into place.

For some hidden and probably neurotic reason my morning shower is my favorite praying place. Perhaps there is something symbolic about it. Maybe I hope that all of my sins and my paranoid thoughts from the day before will be washed away. At any rate, it is a private time away from Jeanette, children, and *usually* grandchildren. It is a time to be alone with that close friend, God.

There is something about talking with a friend that close. It is something we have all experienced, something called "getting it all off your chest." I am not sure why this works so well, but it does. Maybe, when you try to explain yourself completely to someone you trust, you get a whole new picture of you.

I am a person who doesn't easily pour out his troubles to anyone. Sometimes I think I was born suspicious, distrustful. Yet I find it easy to dump those problems on God, because I trust him absolutely. He won't have a fit of temper or a moment of spite and tell my wife what I said in confidence. Instead he listens, and listens with far more love and understanding because he knows me. He created me. For 20 years I have "leaned" on him and told him about my hurt feelings, about those little things that get so big when people are close.

I don't know how God operates. I don't know what he does about the problems we bring to him. I guess I am not even curious anymore about how he responds to his friends. All I know is that he does it well. Over the years I've watched my big problems with Jeanette grow smaller as I told him about them. Many of them disappeared.

So love God first? Why not, when loving him brings so many rewards? Where else can I find a totally reliable friend who always wants love to increase rather than diminish?

How in the world can I even live with myself without making God my closest friend? I am a bigger and better person than I was on the day I married Jeanette, yes, but what a way I have to go! I wake up each morning so depressed that I feel the world will surely go to hell today. We've faced so many unpaid bills in our lifetime that I know another financial disaster awaits us just around the corner, even though we no longer owe anyone anything, and we've never been hungry a day.

I need reassurance. And in whatever way he does things like that, he gives it to me. I come

out of that shower most mornings more confi-
dent than I went in. Somehow, too, he always
finds time in his busy schedule when I need him
during the day. Frequently I take a "reassurance
break" and say to him, "Hey, God, I've found
something else to worry about." I'm not sure
that he laughs with me, but I am sure that he
helps me laugh at myself. After my little chat
with him, I can go back to work with more confidence.

Why not love God first, when it is so good
for me? Like all human beings, I suppose, I am a
mess of feelings. One of those feelings is guilt. I
have my fair share of guilty feelings because I
deserve them. In my younger, "success-oriented"
days, I cheated people, hurt their reputations,
lied to them. The numbers of people I have
damaged with my sarcastic tongue give me a
closet full of the bones and blood of onetime
friends that haunt me constantly. I wish I could
do my life all over again, but I can't.

So what do I do about all that guilt? Blow up?
Crouch in a corner in someone's mental institu-
tion where I am no good to anyone? Do I right
all of the wrongs I have caused and so get rid of
all that guilt? Some of the people I have harmed
are dead and buried; some I don't know how to
find; some I don't even remember. So I ask him
to help me sort out all of this guilt and decide

what to do with it. I know he designed me for something better than saying, "Oh, what a mess I am!"

I find God very picky about guilt. In whatever way he communicates with me (and I don't know how he does that either), he lets me know that there are two kinds of guilty feelings I have to deal with: the kind that I can do something about, and the kind that I can't. He never quite gets off my back about the things I *can* do something about. If I have an apology to make, somehow that thought is always close to the top of my mind. I may rant and rave and say, "She hurt me more than I hurt her!" But after the ranting and raving is over, the thought is still there, "You have an apology to make."

He doesn't even let me completely off the hook about the guilt I can't do anything about. Somehow when I have deliberately or carelessly hurt one of those other people he loves, he wants me to make amends. When I meet a new face that needs something from me, he shows me an old face that I have cheated or destroyed or ig-nored. He seems to be saying, "Here is your chance to balance your scales in favor of love." And he is quick to reward. No sooner have I done something for another that I *know* is good, than the thought takes hold of me: "You are not such a bad person after all, Urb!"

I have many friends, but none like God.

Neighbors. Love them as you love yourself.
A large part of loving myself is loving Jeanette.
As Christ so accurately stated, when we marry in
love we do become one flesh. When I wound
her, I bleed too. When I make her bigger, I feel
bigger.

So Jeanette is my most important neighbor.
If I pretend to love others while ignoring her, I
am giving those others a neurotic and ineffectual
love. All that I am trying to do is make up for
the loss I feel in myself.

But she is not my only neighbor, and I am
not hers. If we try to keep our love to ourselves,
that love will always disappear.

We are close to a couple who do love each
other deeply. They are quite different. They com-
plement each other beautifully and need each
other so much that what one thinks and feels is
the most important thing in the world to the
other.

But, somehow, their experiences in life have
caused them to read love backward. They are trying to do something with love that is impossible
to do. They are trying to keep it all for
themselves and for their children.

We have observed this couple for so long
that we can almost predict when their love is going to turn in on them and become rancid and
stale. Both of them have been hurt by love, so
both are afraid to honestly try loving others.

Both understand what a powerful thing their own love is. Both honestly believe they should do their loving at home and not risk that love with others.

Most couples have their ups and downs, but this one is on a roller coaster. They draw into themselves, and for a time it is beautiful. They say to themselves: "We have our home, the most important place in the world. Let's concentrate on that home. We don't need anyone else."

Except—they do need others. As they shut out that bad old world outside, they have no agenda to occupy them except what is inside. There is just too much of each other, and not enough others. Slowly, they begin to withdraw from each other, too. The situation in the home becomes more lonely, until one or both admit,"We've got to find some friends."

They find some friends. Briefly, they are much happier. But, because they have been alone so long, they expect and demand too much from their new friends.Then those friends disappoint them in some way, and they draw back into themselves—and down they go toward the bottom of love again.

I guess I am being a bit dishonest here. I said I was describing one couple that we know. Actually, I feel sure I am describing about a third of all couples, everywhere. Perhaps I am even talking about all of us at some point in our lives. Jeanette and I have chosen to back away from other people at times. When we have done that, we have also seen our love fall on its face.

"You must love your neighbor as yourself." What a simple statement of fact that is! You can observe this fact by looking around you, not condemning, just looking and learning. I think you will find another third of the couples you know loving their neighbors instead of themselves. One or both are very involved in things outside their home. They belong to many church or civic organizations. They "do good" in a half dozen clubs. They are always looking for "fun things"—running, running, running toward others to avoid themselves. If you look closely, about all you will see in these couples is the fine edge of panic—a great, but honest fear that love will collapse around them if they ever stop running.

But I hope you can also get to see that other third who have finally recognized the wisdom of following the Man's command exactly. They love their neighbors as themselves. They build love in the home and then go out and build it in the people around them. When they get hurt they don't back off, but go out and try to build love again. And here, in these couples, you'll see happiness.

I, I, We, We—I find these words repeated far too often in this book for my own comfort.

Maybe I'm like the man in the Gospels who stood in front of the temple and said, "I thank you, Lord, that I am not like the rest of men. . . ." And sometimes, when I look back at what I have written, I laugh at myself with this thought: "Sometimes this book looks like a soap opera, *The Perils of Urb and Jeanette.* Do they really have a marriage that glows? How about those skeletons in the closet? Will their marriage even survive until the end of the book?"

In other words, this book is far more personal than Jeanette and I intended it to be. And yet we can find no other way of saying what needs to be said. We believe that the real experts in any marriage are the partners themselves. Jeanette and I can't offer a system for loving simply because it will not work for everyone. We are all far too different to conform to anyone else's mold. All we can offer is this: "We have a marriage that works very well. It is a long way from perfect, but we do have a lot of love. Here are the mistakes we believe we have made; here are the things we think we are doing right; here are the things we know we are doing right."

And one of the things we know we are doing right is this: We always try very hard to treat each other as persons. I no longer believe that Jeanette is just something called a woman, or a good wife, or even a female. I've tried to treat her like all of these things, and it was a disaster.

She doesn't fit anyone's nice, neat category—and neither does your wife or husband. She is uniquely Jeanette. And she has made the same kind of discoveries about me.

Through hard experience, we have learned the truth of that rule of Christ's, "So always treat others as you would like them to treat you." There is no baloney here. No pat formula that says, "Treat any woman, 1, 2, 3; treat any man 1, 2, 3—and then the world will be good again."

Instead, if you think about this idea of Christ's, you will be able to see that it is real, because people are real. It changes as people change. I have to learn to ask myself each morning, "What does Jeanette need from me today?" And perhaps, even more important, I have to constantly ask myself, "What do I really need from her?" Jeanette is a person. I am a person. Both of us are children of God and persons of immense dignity. Regardless of our sex, we both need basic, human things: attention, affection, respect, honesty, caring, a loving sexual life and even discipline.

"So always treat others as you would like them to treat you" is a beautiful rule because it again requires that we throw out the garbage we have been taught about love, and about men and women. We start all over through listening and learning. Instead of answers, it offers us a constant search for the answer of how to love that other, and how to become more loveable ourselves. In other words, this rule is the only one that fits the human experience in marriage. A good marriage is not unending bliss. Instead, it is a constant, changing, exploring, improving journey toward mature love.

We rediscovered that golden rule when all of our phony rules for treating husbands and wives had failed us. Our hope is that you will think enough about what you read here to carefully reexamine that rule, if you haven't already.

When I reexamined it I found out a lot of things about myself that I had always vaguely known, but had never faced up to. My most important discovery was this: It doesn't take a lot of things to make me happy. But there are a few things I can't do without:

—I must feel that I am important to someone, because, as a child of God, I am important. Someone has to help me feel my own importance, my own dignity; someone has to help Jeanette feel important. Then there will be two important and more loving people in our home.

—Words and signs of endearment are things that I must have. I need them often, because I find it so hard to believe that I really am a "dear." I need someone to wait on me now and then, someone to give me special attention, someone to say "I love you" over and over again until I finally believe it.

Is that a "masculine" or a "feminine" trait? No, it isn't. Jeanette must have the same things, too, so that she can know that "someone really loves me." She needs to be waited on now and then. She needs to hear "I love you" often.

—I need someone I can depend on; someone who will be behind me, supporting me on those days when I am down in the dumps and can't seem to get up; someone to encourage me when I need encouragement, push me when I need a push, ridicule me, if necessary, when I am acting in a ridiculous way. Someone who will stand by my side when my life is falling all around me and who will still be at my side when the calamity is over and we begin to clean up the debris. When my mother died and I felt very depressed because I hadn't been a loving son, Jeanette was there, patiently listening to me as I talked it through.

But we have to be able to depend on each other and find the support that we all sometimes need in the daily, routine things we do, too. The other day we played a little scene at the dinner table that has become quite common in our home. Jeanette has assumed responsibility for the cooking, not because she is a woman, but because she loves to cook. Sometimes the chore of figuring out menus three times a day, a hundred times a month becomes overwhelming. So she said to me: "I plan to bake this afternoon. Is there anything special you would like for dessert?" I named a half dozen things—apple pie, cinnamon rolls, chocolate cake. Then I told her I like just about everything she bakes. So for supper she made an apple cake, something I hadn't even mentioned. She didn't want to be told what to do; she just needed someone to support her as she faced the often monotonous and sometimes overwhelming task of too many menus.

—Even at age 60, one of the things I need from Jeanette is a satisfying sexual life. Over the years my definition of satisfying sex has changed a great deal, of course. I like to think that a man who has often been satisfied is much easier to satisfy. But then, maybe I'm just getting older.

But according to our golden rule, if I need that satisfaction to be happy, I must provide her with that same satisfaction. And that means always staying in touch with her because her sexual needs, like everything else about her, are changing from day to day. She is not the person I married. I am not the person she married. Events, hurts, experiences, operations and celebrations have changed us both, and will continue to change us both. If we live to be 90, I am sure that both of us will need a satisfying sexual life. But the dimensions of that life are still in the future, yet to be discovered and talked over.

—So perhaps the thing I need the most from her is to be respected and listened to. That may be the most important thing that I can give her. What she says to me is important to her, even when she just rambles on about the minor events of her day. And the smallest things she says are equally important to me, and to my happiness. Some things she seems to repeat over and over, as I do, and these can become very monotonous to listen to because they seem to be always the same. But they aren't the same, because as she listens to me, and I listen to her, both of us change a little. And all of that listening is the only clue that I have about what she is thinking and about who she is, today.

Is it easy to follow the rule "So always treat others as you would like them to treat you"? Of course it isn't. All of us have been carefully trained to respond to all others automatically. We've been taught a whole set of rules for treating medical doctors, another set of rules for "the poor," and a host of rules for treating "men" and "women" and "children." Each of us knows a slightly different set of rules. It is tough to change lifelong habits.

But you have lived with a man or a woman for a while. Let me ask you these questions: Is the way you are treating each other now working? Does the person you have married fit into any nice, neat category? Have you seriously tried giving that other person those same, good, basic things that can make you genuinely happy?

That golden rule is not an easy one to follow. It means looking deeply at yourself, and deciding what you really need from life and from marriage. It means listening to your partner carefully, and always. And when you fail or forget, going back and apologizing and listening again.

Yet I honestly believe that you must make this the second rule of your life in order to build any truly loving relationship. You are different from any other person in this world in many ways. So is your partner. Neither one of you conforms to anyone's pattern. Your marriage doesn't either.

So there is no alternative to constantly searching yourself to discover what you need to be loved. There is no alternative to deeply, carefully observing your partner so that you can discover who that person is, and how you can best give him or her the same good things you need for your own happiness.

Two Rules: Love God; love those around you and yourself. Think about yourself, and about those things that make you truly happy. Then make sure you give those same good things to others. Christ's laws of love are always tough, but never complicated. Little children grasp them quickly. The simple people of this world see the sense of his rules at once.

Maybe our most fervent prayer should be, "O Lord, uncomplicate me!"

7

Talk When It's Fun:
Really Talk When It Isn't

Marriage is a continuing creation of loving people. It is building beautiful, lasting and always growing friendship. We commit ourselves to becoming more loveable, loving and loved when we marry. We talk honestly about everything and we work on establishing some trust, some respect, some acceptance.

The home we build can and must be the place where we gather strength, build confidence in ourselves and in our love. There we can win many small victories over selfishness and dishonesty, and slowly become the kind of persons we want to be.

The tool we use to build loving relationships and loving homes is communication. Though it sounds complicated, communication simply means getting across a very important message to another. That message is "I love you. I need your love. I want you to love me."

Once we succeed in getting this simple message across, the rest falls in place. When I hear clearly "I love you," I also hear all kinds of other things. I hear "someone loves me so I must be a pretty good person after all." I hear "she loves me, so she is not trying to hurt me when she is critical. Perhaps I should listen." I hear "she loves me, so it is safe to give my love in return."

All these things are the things we want out of life. They are the things we need to feel good about ourselves and be happy. Happiness increases as love increases, and the love we build slowly becomes a new part of us that touches everything we do and affects all others we touch.

It is not that hard to say clearly: "I love you. I need your love. I want you to love me." As a matter of fact, it is the natural thing to do. All of the feelings and emotions and sexual drives built into us by a loving God demand that we give and receive love. The only thing that stops us is our phony training. So again, showing love and saying love and doing love are not a learning process, but an unlearning one.

114

What is it that makes it so hard to talk in a loving way? Is it because we have never been trained to talk, never gone to school for communications? That doesn't make sense, because some of the most loving couples are people with very little education. And some of the most unloving, sarcastic and cutting people are highly educated, highly trained in communications skills.

Recently we've come to know two couples who illustrate what I am trying to say. Couple one is highly educated. As a matter of fact, both are educated in communications. Both have graduate degrees that certify them as "Expert Communicators."

We stayed with this couple for three days. They are beautiful to watch; a textbook example of what communications should be. They did everything "right." They "reinforced" one another constantly. They listened to one another attentively, creatively. When she said something to him, he did not blandly assume that he understood what she was saying. He would respond to her in this way: "I think I hear you saying. . . ." And then, on the last night of our visit, she said to him, "If you listen to me creatively one more time, I am going to hit you in the mouth with this bowl of soup."

Now listen to couple two's simpler conversation. John, a little overweight, is helping himself to a second piece of pie. Mary says to him: "Now, John, you know you don't need that second piece of pie. You're too fat already, and it ain't good for your heart." Then she turns to us and says (making sure that John hears her), "I got to keep after that man all the time. I want to keep him around for a while. *Good men are hard to come by.*"

"Good men are hard to come by." I want you, I need you, I love you. Is that so hard to say? Not for John and Mary. Not for all of us—if we are willing to look ourselves over and change the things in ourselves that keep us from saying "I love you." Most of us, too, have to work just as hard to change the things that keep us from hearing "I love you."

It is hard to say "I love you" when so many experiences in life have taught us to "be careful! You've been hurt before, and you can be hurt again. Wait until you are sure he (she) loves you, and then you can safely give your love in return."

It is hard to hear "I love you" when these messages come through from your growing-up years: "You're not good enough." "Why can't you be like Johnny?" "You're worse than your father." "I don't know why you even bothered turning in that paper." "You're a sinner." "You're a bad girl." Hard to believe we are loveable until we look ourselves over and accept ourselves as we are, children of God, persons of immense dignity, but with some things we need to change and improve.

It was hard, too, for Jeanette to hear "I love you" from a man whose chief conversational tool was sarcasm—who always made "humorous" comments (at her expense) about the way she cooked, the way she walked, the way she dressed.

How about your home? Have you ever wondered why your partner has such a hard time speaking to you? Why he or she is so silent, pouts so much? Could it be that you too are good at sarcasm? That your partner is afraid to say what he or she really thinks or feels, because you always respond with a put-down?

Is it possible that you are so unsure of yourself that you pretend to have all of the answers? Have you been taught that men are superior to women (or that women are superior to men) and do you act that way?

Or are you so unsure of yourself that you are always putting on the "humble" act ("It's all my fault. I know I'm wrong.")? That can drive your partner crazy, too. No one is always wrong, and your partner certainly knows that he or she is not always right. You have to say what you really think and feel.

We like to think that we are our own invention—that I am my own man, that she is her own woman—that we are not influenced by what has gone before. But are we? Or are we creatures of habit? Haven't our communications habits been formed long before we married?

There are a lot of "strong, silent types" in American homes, people who drive their partners to distraction because those partners never know what they are thinking. Do they deliberately withhold their thoughts? Have they already been defeated and hurt in attempts at conversation? Are they afraid of being defeated again?

There are also a lot of "compulsive talkers" in American homes. Why do they yak all the time, and so often about nothing? Why are they afraid of silence? Why do they automatically try to dominate most conversations? Why do they listen so seldom? Could it be that they are afraid of what they might discover about themselves?

Almost everyone feels sorry for himself or herself at some time. Feels that "I am the only one who is trying to make this marriage work." Isn't that a habit formed when we thought that the members of our family or our friends didn't care about us?

Conditioning. Training. What a terrible force we let it become in our lives. We let it stop us from saying those simple words: "I love you. I need you. I want you to love me." We watch the movies, we watch TV, and many of us watch our parents. They condition us in a subtle way.

We learn that married people talk about bills, about getting ahead, and about children. Single people talk about love and romance.

The strength of this conditioning was brought home forcefully to us some years ago. Jeanette and I were sitting comfortably on the davenport, and I had my arm around her. Our two teen-age daughters came in with some friends and found us enjoying the holding. The friends looked startled, and after they left one of them said to our daughters, "What's with your mom and dad? Aren't they married?"

Some of us have even had the humanity bred out of us. God created all of us with both reason and strong emotions. Apparently he believed that both of these were good, and that we would need both reason and strong emotions to build love. In other words, those strong emotions are a gift from God, *not* a curse, and he trusts us to use them intelligently. Yet a great many of us have trouble expressing strong emotions. We feel ashamed of them.

Anger is an emotional gift from God, and an insight Jeanette and I have gained through our years of counselling is that its suppression can wreak havoc in a marriage relationship. We believe that God wants us to have the capacity for anger. There are many things in this world that need changing, and they might be changed if and when someone gets angry enough to do something about them.

Yet someone carefully taught most of us that anger was a terrible sin. I suppose all organizations tend to stress this sinfulness because an angry person can be a disrupting force in a classroom, church or home. In school, too, the message came through: Anger is uncivilized, an expression of ignorance; educated people solve their problems through intelligent discussion.

And some people do manage to suppress their anger. But they also have ulcers, heart attacks or severe headaches. They turn their anger in on themselves.

For 35 years I tried to stamp out my anger. What a useless, destructive effort! Anger is a part of me. The more I tried to suppress it, the more it broke out in unexpected and harmful directions. I found myself being angry at the wrong people for the wrong reasons. Just when I thought I had my anger under control, I would find myself spanking my children when there was nothing serious to spank them for.

Anger, like any emotion, can be channeled in useful, constructive directions. Like dynamite, it is useful for blowing up stumps and old bridges, but you can't hide it away in your basement next to the stove and pretend that it doesn't exist.

My own anger led me back to Christ in a kind of final desperation. I could find no answers in my church, because anger always seemed to be wrong there. The only question was the degree of its sinfulness. Prayer was no help, either, because I prayed the way I was taught: "O God, help me get rid of this anger!" Now I think of this prayer as a kind of blasphemy. God gave me the gift of anger, a beautiful gift that can serve me and serve him.

This second look at Christ was a real eye-opener. What I saw in him helped me begin to make sense out of me and out of my counselling as well. Here was a man who wasn't a bit afraid of his anger. He did not apologize for it. His temper caused him to knot a rope and clear the temple when it was the only way to make people understand that God's house was a house of love and not a flea market. Christ let his anger run when he was confronted with the hypocrisy of the Pharisees. He told them exactly what they were in language tougher than most of us have ever used on anyone. What Christ has said to me is this: "Your anger is OK; my father put it there. I have it, too. Use it when it needs to be used, and you won't have trouble with it anymore."

Anger is a part of conflict. But it isn't conflict that kills a marriage. Conflict is always there. Instead it is fear of conflict; or it is confrontation in a halfhearted way.

Before any good marriage can grow up, it has to lock itself in a room and stay there until a man and a woman want to come out and love and be loved again. If I want someone to deeply love me, I have to be willing to put all of myself into that someone. Somewhere in every home we have to confront each other with a kind of total honesty. We have to confront each other with all our hurts, misunderstandings, misinterpretations—even our hatred and the reasons for that hatred. And if we run away before it is settled, we've lost it all. We haven't been willing to pay the price of love.

What actually happens when we begin to confront each other, and then one of us backs off? Most of us know all too well what happens, because nearly every couple plays and replays that silly game. When we hurt each other, and hurt again, and then quit because it hurts too much, both of us are left hurt, insulted, humiliated, frustrated and angry. That frustration cooks inside and burns out our guts with ulcers, high blood pressure, colitis and heart attacks. Or it explodes in useless, destructive directions. There are so many things that you still need to hear.

Strangely, that thing that we fear so much,

that all-out, stay-with-it-until-it's-done kind of quarrel, lasts only a little while longer.

Again, it is a beautiful provision from a God who loves us, for those of us who are willing to invest our total selves in love. If we can only disregard the stupid things we have been taught about confrontations, our own bodies will tell us what will happen if we lock ourselves in a room and stay there and even scream and holler until something is settled. We are all aware of our "emergency glands" and of how they operate. In moments of extreme danger, adrenalin pumps into our bodies and causes us to operate at full tilt. All of our senses are keyed and alert. We talk louder, cry easier, exaggerate terribly. In that moment of extreme danger, our bodies will do anything to protect themselves.

Total confrontation is an extremely dangerous time. Violence is always possible. Someone can get hurt, especially if frustration has been stored up too long. But it is not nearly as dangerous as the continuous pick-and-run-type quarrels that most of us have. A total confrontation *ends* tension and *begins* healing. The greater danger in any confrontation is ending it before everything is said that needs to be said.

The adrenalin will only keep us operating at a fever pitch for so long. Slowly our bodies and our minds begin to run out of gas. And that is when beautiful things begin to happen in a marriage.

Because we are good people with only learned garbage that is bad, something else always happens as the total confrontation begins to wind down. We all exaggerate terribly when the adrenalin is pumping. If I am upset with the way my wife takes care of the house I am liable to call her a slob. If a woman suspects her husband of an evasion, she will certainly call him a liar. But as the "fighting glands" subside, we begin to *hear* ourselves making those outsized exaggerations. So we say: "I went a little too strong. I didn't really mean it. . .," and the healing begins.

We also have gathered the facts we need. Now we have an idea of what it will take to make love glow. We know what that other can't stand about us. We have told each other clearly, plainly, forcefully. It is all outside now, where we can see it and do something about it.

If you haven't already discovered the answer to saying "I love you; I want you to love me," look at Christ's teaching with me again. His first conversations were not about love, because he knew that few of us are ready for that. Something has to come before love in our lives. He calls that something repentance.

A strange word, a "churchy" word. But the meaning of that word was clear to those who wanted to listen. Repentance is simply the process of looking ourselves over and cleaning out the garbage that keeps us from giving and receiving love. He says it is a tough process.

First face ourselves honestly, the good and the ridiculous that is us. When we clear the board out of our own eyes, then we can clearly see the speck of dust in another's.

The person of me is good, because, as a little child once said, "God made me, and God don't make no junk." But the image I have of me is often ridiculous. Either I pump myself up so high that I don't dare look at any of the faults in me, or I hold myself so low that I have no love to give.

For most of us, two kinds of repentance are necessary. I suppose we can call these "positive," and "negative." Positive repentance is a kind of apology to God for running ourselves down. When I say to myself, "No one could possibly love me," I am directly insulting God. I am saying to him, "You sure made a mess of things when you created me." That is never true. We may be a mess, but that didn't come from God. It came from people and from organizations that had a vested interest in keeping us unsure of ourselves and unworthy.

The second kind of repentance can be called

125

negative. Here, in the presence of the Man who knows us, we look ourselves over day by day and hour by hour. We try to discover what it is in us that keeps us from saying, "I love you; I need your love." We also try to discover the things in ourselves that drive our loved ones away. Then comes that tough, and sometimes humiliating experience of apologizing to that loved one, of trying to explain why we have hurt him or her, of asking forgiveness, and of even asking for help in making those changes in us that will make love grow again.

Really, that is what marriage is all about. It is about two people leaning on each other as they slowly grope for something called maturity. It is about long and endless hours trying to explain ourself to that other, and in the process, not only coming closer to our partner, but also slowly learning more about ourself. Marriage is a lifetime of this "repentance." It is working together to rid ourselves of the things that keep us from loving as we were designed to love.

Christ told us that a great secret of love is to talk to one another in simple language. How different this is from what some of us have been taught. Perhaps that is why so many people who lack formal education seem to achieve a beautiful relationship. They speak to each other in language that is common to both of them, the only language they know.

126

Recently Jeanette and I sat in our living room with a minister and his wife. Their marriage was in desperate trouble, and we were acting as referees. One of their problems was immediately apparent. He spoke to her in minister-seminar language, and she had no idea what he was talking about. She thought he was trying to put her down. It wasn't true. He was just talking as a highly educated minister talks.

But it is not just the educated among us who have to overcome language barriers. All of us who work, read, or even watch a great deal of television tend to develop a jargon of our own.

Across the street from us is a railroad man, a beautiful person. But he spent his life talking with mostly other railroad men. He sprinkles ordinary conversations with so many "hot boxes" and "deadheads" that every once in a while I have to say to him: "Hey, boy, back off! I don't know what you are talking about." We take these same habits into our homes and then wonder why we have trouble communicating.

An important part of repentance is forgiveness. Christ instructed us to forgive seventy times seven times. Four hundred and ninety times rolls around in a hurry in most of our homes. Forgiveness is tough, and it's tough for two reasons: we don't bother to explain ourselves, and we take affronts personally. A husband comes home from work like a bear and his wife never stops to think that 10 different people have put him in his sour mood. Instead, she thinks, "What have I done to offend him?" Or even, "He doesn't love me."

Christ's teaching is not just a series of slogans we like to quote. Instead, it is one beautiful, practical, well-assembled package for loving. Do say to yourself, "How would I like to be treated now?" and, "Maybe I had better look first at me, and then perhaps it will be easier to forgive my mate." Walk in the shoes of a woman who is raising children, keeping house, and perhaps holding down a job, and it is easier to understand why she may be ornery and quarrelsome.

If you honestly look yourself over you will see that Christ's ideas for forgiveness are practical. In many cases there really is nothing to forgive. A huge percentage of the problems between a husband and wife begin when one or the other is temporarily out of control because of what Kathy Connell describes as "all that stuff."

It builds up on some days. Your sinuses act up; your friendly banker is unfriendly about an overdraft; you know there is something physically wrong and you are worried sick. Those are the days when you have "keep-off" signs all over you. You deserve forgiveness and so does your mate.

In theory, at least, it shouldn't be hard to

forgive even adultery. One person sometimes commits adultery in a marriage, but very often both bear some responsibility for it.

I think about Jeanette during our hurting times. Think about the fact that I gave her almost none of the things that a woman needs to feel loved and important and good about herself. I also think of the fact that I did give her plenty of the things that make a woman feel lonely, and put-upon, and vengeful. At times she must have been literally starved for affection—even for a single kind word from a man.

I think about myself during those tough times, doing what a marriage counselor often does—sit in an office talking with women about their sex problems. I think about how some of them responded to a professionally kind and understanding man, remember the thought that often crossed my mind—"Lady, we could be a great help to each other." If it is true that we commit adultery in our hearts then I am guilty, and believe that almost every married person is also guilty.

Even adultery is basically "all that stuff." All that stuff that keeps us from doing what we want to do and what we married to do—love each other fully and completely. It is hurt feelings and poor training and saying "I will love you when you love me."

Practical Christ knew about adultery and

forgave it. He said that under his new law of love, we should forgive it too, and that it was our "hardened hearts" that kept us from doing so. Perhaps adultery should be forgiven as a form of temporary insanity.

You have an idea now of how strongly I believe in the power of love. It is stronger than the temptation to cheat, and much stronger than the devil. Once real love touches a pair of lives, it stays in those lives, will survive almost anything and still be ready for rebuilding.

Marriage counseling has taught me the reality of this immense power. I have seen couples come close to killing each other, but still they ask: "Help us to stop hurting each other. We don't want to break this up. No one can tell us we have fallen out of love." People can lose their respect for each other; they can even hate each other, but I don't believe they "fall out of love."

It saddens me to see the many divorces that happen because people don't trust or develop their love. There are literally hundreds of precipitating reasons that "cause" divorce, but if real love was once present then the underlying cause is that one or both of the partners was afraid to put it all in. One or both chose to run rather than stay and fight it through with everything they had.

There was a time in my life when I actually condemned people who initiated a divorce. But now I condemn the actual villain, that misguided training of ours that keeps us from confronting each other with all of the feelings and emotions and hurts that are in us.

This, then, is the kind of hardheaded, tough-loving communications I find through Christ. That is why he is the only expert I really listen to, because he is the only one who is always real.

We learn a pasty-faced, take-what-you-can-and-run, tricks-and-gimmicks, sexual-acrobatics kind of love from this world of ours. These things work only up to a point—a point that we all hit—where loving gets tough.

It is here that we hear that quiet insistence of his: "Don't give me that Lord, Lord business. Go make things right with your partner. If your partner won't listen to you, take a friend along, someone you both trust. Go see a priest, or a minister, or someone who cares about you both."

I always hear practical things in Jesus Christ—things like patience, persistence, and walking that extra mile. I hear a man who talks about love as it is, about the tough road it has to follow, and then tells us about the great rewards at the end of that road.

Some of you may be turned off by the "religious stuff" you read in this book. Some of

131

you may be saying to yourself, "I had that Jesus thing poured into me right up to my neck when I was a kid. What I need now is something practical. All Jesus is interested in is salvation and ministry and things like that."

Don't you believe it. Maybe the human beings who told you about Jesus made him an otherworldly type. If that has happened to you, go look at him again.

8

Don't Clutter Up Your Lives

One of the most troublesome and puzzling aspects of the gospels for this thoroughly modern man has been Christ's insistence on simplicity. He speaks to us early in his ministry about the happiness we will find if we discover the will of his Father and then follow it. But then he seems to spoil it all by asking us to get rid of all the intricate and complicated things that "everyone knows" lead to happiness.

This insistence on simplicity is not just a one-time thing with Christ. Apparently he deeply believes that the less we complicate our lives, the happier we will become. At least a dozen times, and perhaps 40 (I haven't counted them), he repeats the idea, "Get rid of that excess baggage!"

He tells a rich man to sell all he has and give it to the poor and then follow his way. He speaks about the birds of the air, and how uncomplicated their lives are. He urges us to talk in simple language, to pray in simple language. He speaks often about things that rust out, and things that wear out, and about the unnecessary worry and tension we create for ourselves when we build our lives around those things.

It amuses me now that I once thought that all of these references to simplifying our lives were "spiritual," a call to deny ourselves everything, to suffer a lot here and now so we could "lay up treasures in heaven." Now I know that practical man was again speaking about the here and now. He was saying something that is absolutely true. To a point, the less we have, the less we have to worry about.

Some people have interpreted his words to mean that the best way to achieve happiness is to totally sacrifice all material things and go off to a monastery someplace. But I don't read him that way. There are certain minimums that all of us need to be happy. Even after Christ's death the apostles were out in their boats fishing. They had their families to support and their dignity and pride to maintain. They owned their boat and they owned their nets and he showed his approval of what they were doing by helping them find the fish they needed.

But beyond these basic things, how much do we need to be happy? Each family will have to answer that question in a different way. But a little thought about your own experiences in living will convince you that Christ is right: The more that you accumulate, the more you have to worry about.

And when we spend more time worrying, we have less time for loving and building love, the one thing in life that always yields happiness.

I'd like to say that in one more way, and then give you some examples to think about:

The more complicated we make our lives, the more complicated it is to live those lives—and we again have less time for building love.

We decide to buy a car. The purpose of a car is to go from here to there. There isn't much we can do about owning a car in America today. Over the years our country has made its choices. Practically all means of going from here to there have been eliminated, except for the car. And most of us live so far from where we work and shop that we have to have that car.

But what kind of car? This will be a big investment. We've been taught to go to the experts for advice on all major decisions. We go to the experts on cars (the people who sell the cars, make loans for them, insure them, or service them). All agree: "Get a car that has everything on it that will add to your pleasure and comfort. This will increase your happiness with your car."

You get your new car and it is wonderful. The horn whistles "Dixie," if that is the option that makes you happy. The air conditioner keeps you cool on hot days and the heater keeps you warm on cool days. Two separate brake systems keep you safe. Windows go up and down without the strenuous effort of cranking them. Headlights disappear when you touch a button. You open the trunk electrically from the inside. Power steering helps you steer and power brakes stop you smoothly. Some get the pleasure of saying to a neighbor, "My car has got more stuff on it than your car does."

But shortly, you run into the Rule of Automatics: *The more complicated a machine is, the more parts there will be to break down.* Parts begin to break down and your worry and tension increase. You have to pay to fix them. You become irritable, snap at your wife, blame her for misusing the car, and suggest she take driving lessons. You worry about going to the supermarket, because you are driving a high-priced piece of machinery, and supermarket parking lots are notorious places for high-priced pieces of machinery to get creamed. If that happens, you or your wife will have to run around to body shops getting estimates. When your car gets back from the body shop, it will be rebuilt and probably worth less than what you still owe on it.

The two of you have a house to furnish. You love your mate, so you think, "We will make this home of ours as comfortable and convenient for each other as we can." Again you consult the so-called experts who sell and service appliances, and who arrange the loans on appliances, and who finance their magazines by advertising appliances. All agree: "Get all of the gadgets you can so that everything can be done in the easiest possible way. And get all of the attachments for all of those gadgets. Then you will be happy."

So you buy a self-cleaning stove with a digital clock and a mini-computer. You have separate gadgets to cook two hamburgers, four hot dogs, and 30 cups of coffee. Out in the yard is a riding lawn mower, a powered snow shovel, and everything else that will make life easy. And again you run into that first Rule of Automatics: *The more complicated a machine is, the more parts there will be to break down.*

Besides, the thing that fries two hamburgers so neatly is a demon to wash. And there isn't enough storage space for all those things, and there are all those payments.

I suppose I am almost simpleminded in my

beliefs about things, and about owning them. If they build genuine love, then they are good. But if they build unnecessary tension, strain, worry, jealousy—if they hurt the love between people—they are stupid.

The same thing can be said about every other part of our lives. If we keep our lives simple, then they will be loving and beautiful. Always ask, "Is this *really* the loving thing to do?"

That's not easy. Most of us have been carefully taught to "listen to the experts" on all things that apply to our lives. But so many of the so-called experts are owned by the corporations that employ them, their own professional organizations, the government, churches or charitable organizations. Perhaps these experts were trained to help us. But that is not their principal goal anymore. We are not the ones who pay their salary. Instead their job is to involve us, to make us ardent supporters of the people who do pay them. They try to persuade us that we need whatever it is they are selling.

One group of "experts" is totally devoted to convincing us that we are tense, worried, put upon and overworked. The motive, of course, is to sell us relaxation. These "experts" have learned how to make us feel either guilty or stupid if we don't relax in the specific way that they recommend. Many of us wonder right now if we shouldn't be out there jogging and, of course, if we shouldn't have purchased jogging suits and running shoes.

These "experts" magnify whatever tension is in us. They inform us of our great need to relax, and then hard-sell us relaxation in any and every form—sleeping aids, cross-country skiing, dinner-at-the-Dells, 10 uninterrupted hours of professional football, weekends with Michelob. They succeed in making us feel sorry for ourselves. And, in some homes, we are so busy relaxing and planning and paying for relaxation, that we have no time for each other—which creates immense tension and worry—and the need for more relaxation.

Another whole group of "experts" is engaged in the business of playing up guilt. Most of this group are, or at least have been, dedicated, concerned, honest individuals who are trying to do something about the real problems that plague people. But in the process of seeking a way to get their messages across they too can find themselves owned by organizations—organizations with budgets, with quotas to meet, reports to file, and in competition with other "helping" organizations.

Many of us then feel guilty because we cannot always help. We learn from them that our children will be deprived unless both they and their parents participate in scouts, little league, dance, music, or a hundred other "opportunities for growth." At the same time the children's parents are also urged to join and be active in a hundred more "good" organizations to "help" their "unfortunate" fellow men. Each of these organizations contains some good, honest, dedicated people. We can benefit both ourselves and others by selectively joining a limited number of them. But a strange thing can happen in many homes. We can become so involved in loving everyone that we have no time left for someone.

I have used this example before, but I think it bears repeating: If I were to die, and were unfortunate enough to go to hell, I am sure the devil would enlist me in his own Family Life Department. This is my area of expertise. Perhaps he would put me in charge of destroying loving homes, and if he did, I am sure he would give me careful instructions. He is not a fool, this devil. He knows that it is not easy to destroy genuine love by tempting those lovers with other men and women. Who's hungry for cake, when he is already loaded with pie?

The devil will know that the best way to destroy lovers is with love. With guilty love. If he should give me that task, I would know exactly how to go about it. I would immediately gather a huge core of "experts in human relationships" (psychologists, social workers, marriage counselors, clergymen, youth counselors). I would instruct each one of them to set up at least one good organization. I would ask them to make sure that all of these organizations were good; you can't tempt honest bankers with counterfeit money.

Next I would set up a huge printing press in hell, and would purchase mailing lists that contained the names of deeply concerned and loving people. I would bombard these caring people with stark pictures of neglected children, starving infants, aborted fetuses, deprived families, battered wives, lost youths popping pills, brutal prisons, ill-equipped hospitals, and migrant workers in fields poisoned by chemicals. Each letter would ask, "What are you doing to stamp out these evils? The Lord needs you in his work!"(I am sure my chief would even authorize a few organizations whose purpose was to make war on the devil, as long as these organizations demanded a great deal of time and involvement. Singlemindedly fighting the devil seems to be a very good way of losing track of love.)

Now, with a huge TV campaign employing movie stars, distinguished citizens and star quarterbacks to endorse our organizations, I could raise the devil in all kinds of homes. I would have the good husbands, wives and children of this world flying in all directions, helping everyone to "mature," and "grow."

And with no time left to even listen to family members, much less love them.

Yet I know the devil would laugh as I un-
folded my great plan for destroying loving
homes. He thought about it a long time ago.

Simplicity: It is worth fighting for. The more
complicated we make our lives, the more complicated it is to live those lives. The simpler our
lives become, the more time we have to concentrate on those things that build love.

Money, clothes, organizations, cars, conve-
niences, relaxation—we need all of these things
to fill our lives. But the basic thing we need for
ourselves, and that others need from us, is love.

Have you talked about uncomplicating your
lives lately?

9

Don't Sell Out Too Cheaply

I want to talk about some words before I finish this book. Some of them are old-fashioned. Words perhaps that appeal to a 60-year-old man. And yet, I think we have to bring them back into fashion and give them some new meanings that apply to our times. So will you bear with me still once more as we review some of the ideas I have stressed throughout this book, using these important words as a starting point?

1. *Adult*—Jeanette and I have heard a lot of definitions for this word; definitions that contain everything from beards, to busts, to drinking

booze at 21. I have also heard more sophisticated definitions that include strong self-image, ability to express emotions, and more. But this is the simple definition that we like: *An adult is a person who accepts responsibility for his or her own acts.*

Age doesn't seem to have much meaning for adulthood. We know quite a few 50-year-old children, and a few 21-year-old adults. A child may say: "I batted the ball, but Johnny didn't catch it. It is his fault that the window broke." A childish woman may say: "I know I look like the wrath of the gods when he comes home at night. But that is his fault. He doesn't notice what I look like anyway." A large-size little boy will often say: "Sure I stop for a drink or two after work. You'd drink, too, if you had to go home to a nag like that."

I did it but it's your fault—the words of a child of any age.

We all flunk this definition of adulthood. We all like to play the game of "See what you made me do." I think, too, that this is one of the reasons so many marriages fail. It is hard to respect and love a person who habitually blames you, mother, government and even God for his or her actions.

2. *Freedom*—Again, there are a lot of definitions of "freedom in marriage." Some of them are insane. We are to let our partners be

"free to do what they want," whether that be moving in and out of marriage, abandoning the children, or establishing sexual relationships with others who can "contribute to their growth."

Jeanette and I both think of freedom in this way: *Allowing and encouraging our partners to become what God has designed them to be rather than what we want them to be.*

Freedom, to us, is approaching marriage with a sense of wonder. It is looking at our lover and asking ourself, "Who is this beautiful person God helped me choose?" It is knowing, or at least trying to know, just one thing about our mate: "You are as good a person as I am."

Freedom is admitting to ourselves that both men and women are made in just one image, and the name of that image is not dad.

And, above all, we think freedom in marriage is a shared thing. It is working out our own marriage, in our own way, with deep respect for each other, and with no respect at all for the many voices who say, "Your marriage has to be this way."

3. *Personal Dignity*—Simple observation will tell us that you and I are the greatest of all animals, that people are the best idea God ever had. The design and construction details for both you and me are different from those of any other person in this world. No matter how he chose to do it, it is nice to know that my Father was so

involved in me, that he put so much thought into what he wanted me to be.

As self-centered as this may seem, I think we all need to reflect long and often on our own great dignity. Knowing who I am and what I can be is not only a comfort to me, it also helps me to see the dignity in you. Knowing that I am both a child and a friend of that immense person named God makes it so much harder for me to cheat you, destroy you or take advantage of you in any way. These foolish acts become "beneath my dignity."

4. *Commitment*—Mature love is built over a long period of time, with many reverses and misunderstandings. But people have to stay there to build this kind of love.

Sometimes, I think, all of us too quickly discard some of our most valuable traditions. As I remember it, I made a very serious and public commitment to my wife that went something like this: "I, Urban Steinmetz, take you, Jeanette Hockers, to have and to hold, for better or worse, for richer or for poorer, in sickness and in health, until death do us part."

Those may not have been my exact words, but they are the ones that most perfectly represent what I believe about commitment in marriage.

I think, if I were a pastor, I would want to talk with young couples for hours about those words. About the having and the holding that must go on forever if they hope to build a loving home.

I would want to talk with them about the better and the worse, and I would feel that it was only fair for them to know how good that "better" can be, and how tough that "worse" may be.

For richer or for poorer, in sickness and in health—I would want them to hear it all, and to look at it all in the married people around them. Until death do us part—I would want them to thoroughly understand that marriage is forever.

If they balked at any of these terms, or wanted to modify them, or refused to listen to them, I believe I would be tempted to hand them a motel-room key and say to them: "This may be a better solution for you than the one you have asked me to witness."

Sex may be the frosting on the wedding cake, but commitment is the ingredient that binds the whole cake.

5. *Discipline*—"He who does not take up his cross and follow me is not worthy of me." Perhaps I am boring my readers by referring to the Gospels again and again, but they are exciting. My life's work is oriented to love—here, now, and specifically in this real home. Christ's words make so much sense for that home, for my home.

The cross I take up when I marry you is you. The cross you take up is me. To follow Christ when we "love one another, as I have loved you," requires discipline. If I am not willing to take on all of the burdens you bring with you, then I am not worthy of you, either. Somehow I have to help you get rid of the things that hurt you. They hurt me, too, because I love you.

6. *Integrity*—Jeanette and I would define integrity this way: *Doing what you know is right, refusing to do what you know is wrong—no matter who (or what) says, "Do it this way."*

So many times we let other people decide what is right and wrong for us. The reason: It seems easier to follow a nice, neat set of rules. And it seems so hard to decide for ourselves. So many things seem half-right and half-wrong. But my mind doesn't live in someone else. It lives in me. That mind of mine won't let me rest until it knows that I am doing what God, if he were present, would want me to do.

I ask myself questions about my own integrity every day. But I don't just ask myself, because I know that in many areas I am "blind in one eye and can't see out of the other." I know that the authorities who tell me, "This is right," and, "That is wrong," are often just as blind as I am. They are people, too. Jeanette has to live with my "rights" and my "wrongs"; I have to live

with them; and both of us have to live with our
God. So the three of us finally decide what is
right and wrong, both for me and for us.

7. *Self-Respect*—All these words lead up to
the most important ones in marriage: Self-
respect. Everything that we are to each other
depends on those two words. If I am going to
love you, I first have to love me. I can't love me
unless I am worthy of love.

All of us sell out too cheaply at many points
in our lives. I can remember, with no pride, putting Jeanette down in front of other phony men,
because I wanted to show them I was "boss."
And some of us sell our souls for a raise in
salary. We all are tempted in the name of
"security." I think the saddest expressions I ever
hear are these: "If I don't take advantage of
this, someone else will," or "My profession
demands . . . " or "You've got to take care of
Number One." The fact of the matter is that
after we have taken care of Number One, we
have to lie there at night with Number One and
somehow live with the kind of person we have
become.

It is certainly easier to live with someone else
if we like the person inside us.

10

Afterthoughts

Ending a book is always a difficult task. A book tends to become a statement about its author and what he or she believes. Naturally the author wants that statement to be both complete and clear, but it is difficult to be sure of achieving either of those things.

So it is nice to be able to add a chapter called "Afterthoughts." Here I can say the things I forgot to say earlier, and re-say the things I may have said badly. These, then, are my thoughts as I finish this book:

About Men and Women

Why do so many people waste so much time trying to define a man and a woman? Christ never bothered with it, so why should we? He never said, "Here are the rules for men—and here are the rules for women." Instead he asked us all to follow the *same* rules. They add up to plain, decent, human treatment.

Some sincere people insist that we follow "God's Plan for Marriage." Now what in the world is that? If God had a special plan just for married people, Christ would have clearly stated it. We can all pick bits and pieces out of a huge Bible and "prove" anything that we want. People have been using the "Word of God" to "keep people in their place" for centuries.

If my friend God is involved in a "plan," it has to be both a workable plan and a loving one. Making a person called a woman the cheerful and always submissive slave of a person called a man is neither workable nor loving.

Christ is the only person in the Bible I completely trust when he speaks about God and about love. He is the only one who is God. All the rest of the people of the Bible were people.

Christ asked us all to be servants of our lovers. He *didn't* say, "You, with the feminine curves, *you're* the servants; and you, with the muscles, you're the masters. . . ." Instead, he told us, "Love one another, as I have loved you." No male rules; no female rules.

Some persons today insist that women be "totally free." I'm in favor of that. Freedom is who I am; freedom to be what God designed me to be is one of my deepest beliefs. I want the same freedom for you, whatever your sex may be.

But what do women actually want? The same "freedom" men have? Men are not free. Instead they are slaves to their own conditioning. If women imitate the phony facades our world asks its men to wear, they will not be free, either. Men are taught from birth to isolate themselves from their fellow men. They are handed a set of rules that make it nearly impossible to love and be loved. Men are taught to win, to dominate, to climb over others. In the thousands of years men have ruled the world, we have created a society not unlike that of cattle in a pasture. We learn to push and butt in an attempt to become Head Bull, no matter how much of our own or others gore we leave behind us.

In our male pasture, we divide ourselves into a phony pecking order. We give each other classifications, titles and degrees that spell out our positions in that pecking order and separate us from one another. We train men to look up to those with superior classifications, and look down on those below them. Even our churches

157

have their own well-established pecking order.

And behind us, as a direct result of our blind urges to rise above others by making them less, are centuries of conflict and killing and fear. Ahead of us is more hate unless we give more than lip service to the teaching of Jesus—that all men are brothers, and those who hope to influence others must become their servants, not their masters.

I get the impression that some feminists would like women to adapt to these same roles. But I doubt that most women are sympathetic to shrill and vengeful voices. There are just too many soft and sensible voices that are saying that we *all* need to be liberated, that all persons regardless of sex or status should be treated as persons of immense and equal dignity.

So men? Women? People. And marriage? A loving, creating, people-building union of a female person and a male one.

As I said in the beginning, I am not at all sure what a man is, or what a woman is. I don't think you are either. So why don't we all relax and find out?

Love Is Worth the Effort

I read a silly article just a few days ago. Some lady was having a fit because some of us have suggested that building love is *work*. She didn't like the word "work." She related it in her mind to drudgery. She wanted love to be beautiful and spontaneous. I do, too.

But it isn't always spontaneous, and sometimes love is drudgery. And building love is always work. If we wait for love to happen, it doesn't happen.

I believe that anyone can have a marriage that sparkles and glows. You can if you know that it is worth the effort, the biggest, most sustained effort of your lives. It *is* worth the effort. Real love doesn't just pay off with a rousing time in bed tonight (although that in itself is worth the building). Love pays off down the road in a lack of fear. When you build love, you also build a safe haven. Your home becomes a place where you can truly be you—with all your anger and frustrations and bitchiness and humor and despair—and know, through all of these, that your home will still be intact and stronger in the morning.

Your sustained effort to build love will even pay off after one of you dies. Jeanette and I know a beautiful older woman whose husband recently died. They hadn't had an easy marriage, because both were strong-minded people who gave themselves and each other a lot of trouble. But they stuck with it and built a deep and permanent love.

That permanent love didn't stop when Jake

died. She misses Jake a great deal, but there is no overwhelming, destroying grief. She doesn't have to live with the thought, "I wonder what it could have been if only I . . . ." Instead this thought keeps her smiling and serene and wondering what tomorrow will bring: "It was tough, but we stuck with it, and we finally had something great." She misses his physical presence, but doesn't feel Jake has left her. That kind of love lives forever.

Recently, our 71-year-old lady friend said to another, bitter woman: "Yes, it is tough learning to live with a man, any man. But it is worth the effort. If the right man came along, I might just decide to do it all over again."

Love Is a Total Package

If you have worked on love in your home as hard as you can and things still don't seem to be working right, have you considered your style of life and how it is affecting that love? Love is not just a man and a woman in one home, keeping the rest of the world outside. Instead love is two persons moving in and out of the home, and acting in ways that either make them loveable or unloveable.

When I am dissatisfied with me, I am critical of Jeanette, and she, of course, is resentful. Usually I find that my feelings about her are only reflections of my feelings about me, and that I have a me to straighten out before I can again have a loving she.

In a very real sense, that is the story of marriage today. Too many of us are trying to do the impossible. We try to make our homes islands of love, while we continue to live in unloving ways. We try to serve two gods; the God of Love when we are together, and the god of the "Real World" when we are apart. It doesn't work.

Love is a total package. It is a 24-hour day. During all of that day, I have to be satisfied with me, so that I can more easily be satisfied with you.

It is easy for me to see what is wrong with other people's marriages. The statistics on divorce are high, and are going to get higher unless there are some great changes in the way so many couples live. By looking around you, you too can see why love isn't working for "some others." Elements of their lives have become real deterrents to building successful relationships.

—In how many of our homes is the booze flowing so freely that it has become the chief concern of all the occupants of that home? The flow of alcohol is a major deterrent to any continuing, coherent conversations about "us."

—How many of us are involved in the total worship of a god called "Monthly Payments"? This is a jealous god who permits no pitter-patter about inconsequential things like building love. He demands that nearly all conversations center on "Monthly Payments." Who is responsible for them? How do we make them? Do we both take second jobs to keep up with them?

—How many of us are so deeply involved and concerned about ourselves that we have no time left for building a relationship? We have made "personal growth" and "self-fulfillment" our gods and follow those gods religiously.

—How many women have elected to become full-time housewives but get so involved in distracting activities that they can do little about *being* housewives? They become so involved in activities, ranging from den-mothering to taking enrichment courses, that they neglect their homes and feed their loved ones on artificial breads and pastries, chemicals and the latest prepackaged garbage foods. And then they wonder why they are losing the respect of their loved ones.

—How many people go to jobs they don't like and do as little as they can? Or how many waste vast amounts of energy in busywork, creating nothing, producing little and leaving nothing behind. Then they come home at night exhausted from their efforts and are tense, unhappy and uncommunicative.

—How many of our helping professionals try to

do others out of more than their share? How many get involved in professional organizations that smother their greedy goals in reams of self-justifying paper that clearly state their great determination to help their fellow humans? Some come to believe their own gibberish and feel noble enough to form professional ethics committees that insure that they will be well-compensated neighbor lovers. How many people engaged in such activities can really like themselves? And how can they then successfully relate to a loved one?

—How many of us have become married to our careers, leaving little or no time for our partners, or letting office and job "things" take precedence over the "little things" that nurture love?

When we talk about "all that stuff" that keeps us from being as loving and as loveable as we want to be, we talk about all of us at some time. It is hard work trying to justify our own unloving behavior; so hard, in fact, that it consumes whatever love that is in us. How do we convince ourselves that it is OK to help produce shoddy merchandise, to help destroy or bankrupt others, to carry home parts in our lunch buckets, to spend our family's security on ourselves, to neglect a commitment to homemaking by escaping to away-from-home activities like the local racquet club, or to convince people they need an unneeded professional service?

Who can ever really believe those phony modern slogans, "If I don't take it, someone else will" or "It goes with the job," or "Look out for number one?"

How can we build loving relationships at home when such behaviors are a part of our daily lives in the "real world"?

Just recently, love stopped working for me as well as it usually does. I have fought my lazy self long enough to know that the problem was probably me. When I talked it all over with my friend God (after ignoring him for several days), I gave him all of my usual excuses: "There is too much work to do; too many promises to keep, and I am 60 years old and the weather outside is beautiful and—"

Then there it was in front of me: too much work to do; too many promises to keep. And none of this was getting done.

Can an ordinary office desk hurt love in my home? Yes, it can, if I sit and read a Western when I should be working at my desk. Can a neighbor with cancer hurt love in my home? Yes, he can, if he needs a visit from me and I stay home and feel sorry for him instead. Can buying a four-wheel-drive car affect the way I treat Jeanette? Yes, it can, if I take advantage of the hard-pressed person who has to sell the car.

Love is a total package of all the things that make me loving or unloving. It is not just me and you. Instead it is an exciting and lively search through all of the people and "all of that stuff" that makes me me and us us.

About Children, Parents, and Parenting

I hate to make children an "afterthought." Yet I have waited until the end of the book to summarize what I believe about them, because this is a book about marriage.

Perhaps, though, children should be an "afterthought" in a marriage. I am not sure I can quote him exactly, but Father Theodore Hesburgh of Notre Dame once said something like this: "The finest thing a father can do for his children is to love their mother." Amen to that. Children deserve to be a product of love, not a product of sex. If I had my "druthers" I would like to see all children arrive in homes where love had already begun to settle down. But since this is unrealistic, I think we have a responsibility to the children we bear to surround them with the love of loving parents as soon as we can.

The question many young couples are sincerely asking today is this one: "Should we have children?" From the perspective of an aging grandparent I can respond just as sincerely,

"You are out of your mind if you can—and you don't." If you firmly decide to commit yourselves to love, each stage of life brings its own loving compensations. Sometimes it is hard for an older person to feel useful and important. It is then that grandkids look up at us with their almost total trust and belief, and tell us with both their words and their actions that grandpa and grandma are some of the most important people in the world. So one good reason for having children is grandchildren—when we need them most and when they need us.

But children themselves are the best reason for having children. Your task of helping them grow up never ends. Their task of helping you grow up never ends. Your children will provide you with excitement and stimulation and grief, with joy and sorrow and anger and frustration, with plenty to forgive and plenty to be forgiven for. In other words, your children will provide you with everything you need to remain thoroughly alive and growing.

What is raising children all about? Each day I am learning a little more about that—from my own children.

But I can say this with a kind of terrible certainty: I wish I had treated each child from birth as I wanted that child to treat me. That same old golden rule. I wish I had always treated each child as a person—like me—rather than as a thing called a "baby" or a "boy" or a "girl."

I am sure, now, that if I had thought of my children as persons like myself, I would never have permitted a stupid medical system to separate me from both my child and his mother at a time when both of them needed me; at the time of birth. Six times I walked out on Jeanette at her moment of greatest pain. I walked out, too, at our moment of greatest joy and pride and shared love.

And I walked out on Bob and Lee, and Millie, and Jim, and Mary, and finally Pete at *their* most terrible moment, at that moment when each of them was torn from a dark, soft, thoroughly comforting womb into a bright, frightening world.

My hands had caressed our babies for nine months while they rested and grew in Jeanette's belly. But they were not there to greet and touch and reassure my newborn child. Instead I let my children fall into the hands of strangers who did rude and professional things to them. And I let those same strangers give Jeanette a "whiff of something" so that she too would not be there to welcome those frightened infants into the world. And I did all this for the stupidest of reasons. The doctor said so.

We even had some of our children *when* we had them for that same reason. Some impersonal professional told us that some patterns of married intercourse were "natural" and some "unnatural." It seemed to me to be unnatural to make love when a thermometer said to make love, but not to when our bodies and hearts and minds needed and wanted to make love. Naturally we got pregnant often playing this unnatural game.

I claim to be an adult. That means I have assumed responsibility for me. But I am also a married adult. That means I am also responsible for the love we produce and for loving the children our love produces. And so is Jeanette. These are our responsibilities.

For too many years I thought of my children in terms of rules to be followed or stages of growth to be suffered through. I'm afraid I thought of them as small animals to be trained rather than as persons to be loved. Too many years I looked at them and said, "This is a child," and forgot, "This is a person, like me, who wants and needs the same things I need."

So, even though my children are all grown up, there are still many years of parenting ahead of me. I listen to people who kiss their children off at a magic age of 18 or 21, and I think to myself, "How can that be?" Perhaps, unlike me, they have done their parenting job totally right the first time. But in my case, and with each of my children in a different way, there is a lot of undoing to do, and a lot of redoing, and even some apologizing.

There is a lot of loving and enjoying to do with my children, too. There never seemed to be enough time for those important things during their growing-up years. Once the apologizing is done, there are many long and pleasant hours of just getting acquainted again, of discovering what these fine young adults hope and believe and want.

There is learning from our children, and pride in that learning. Perhaps Jeanette and I learned to treat each of them as persons a little late in life, but we did finally learn (or, at least, are learning). We no longer see only the mistakes we may have made in loving them. Now we also see some beautiful people emerging. Maybe, we think, a part of that, at least, is us.

Then, there is the marveling. How in the world did these six completely different persons come out of one home? The new ideas each of them presents to us, the different perspectives they form on life, the challenges each issues; the different skills each brings to our family community. Our children, and the people they marry, and the children who result from their love, not only keep us alive and lively, but they give us a kind of immortality as well. Whatever love we can give them, whatever sense of dignity we may be able to impart, or share, or even receive from them will live in someone long after Jeanette and I are dead.

And, finally, parents have a family community to build, a base of caring and mutual support that everyone needs and everyone wants, although they may not know it at the time. Sociologists call this community an extended family, and point out that all stable societies of the past have had these strong, supporting units.

A family community is simply parents, their children and their marriage partners, and the children who result from their love. A family community is a larger group of closely related people doing the same things that build love and happiness in one home, working together to build and maintain and support love in *all* of the family's homes.

Parents are the natural center of any wider family community. Parents never stop trying to build love and encourage love between and among all of those they love. And theirs is not an easy task. People inhabit all of the homes that make up an extended family, and the people we raised in our home are just as human as the people you raised in yours.

New people enter the family community. Bob marries a person called Judy, and Lee marries a person called Denny. Judy is totally different from anyone else in our family; so is Denny, so are the rest of the people who married our children.

Denny and Judy and the rest also come from families. Like all people, they enter this new family a little on the defensive, wondering if they will be accepted. There is a little defiance, too, in all new brides and grooms: "I married my husband (wife), not his family."

And the family "welcomes" this new addition with some mistrust and suspicion. This stranger is "different."

New people bring excitement, conflicts, jealousies, alliances, gossip, hurt feelings, tears—all of the human things that can finally yield greater love and understanding, if the parents stay with it, and if some of the new families mature and understand what the parents are trying to do, and help them. The goal: a beautiful, loving, family community that makes all of its members stronger and supports them when they need support.

So what are parents? They are people who never stop loving their families. They are people who never stop hoping and praying and trying to encourage all of their family members to love one another. As long as parents keep parenting, they stay alive and vital, interested and interesting, and happy with themselves, no matter how tough the loving becomes. When parents stop parenting, they die. Sometimes dead parents

171

live for another 40 years. But there is not much living in a life that says: "It's over, I've raised them. Now I care only about me."

Community. What a beautiful word! Christ built a small community around himself. The apostles argued with each other, violently disagreed, were jealous of each other, laughed together, and through all of this, finally came to know and understand and trust and love one another. Through this unity they developed a power of love that was awesome.

Support Your Marriage With Loving People

This is a strong belief: No marriage can stand alone. People need people. If couples want their marriages to glow and grow in love, they will need the help and support and encouragement of other couples who want the same thing.

That shouldn't be so hard to see if we look honestly and carefully at the forces arrayed against our modern marriages, and especially against those couples who want a loving home. If you want to know how much our society "encourages" love in the home, just look around you. Look at the TV shows and the commercials. Look at the cocktail parties, and the conversations of the boys in the bar—and the girls in the bar. Look at friends who are divorced and the clubs for men and the clubs for women.

A marriage that tries to stand on its own is a lonely marriage. The couple may often wonder, "What's the use? No one cares whether we love each other or not."

What I am trying to say is this: *Everyone needs to belong to a community that cares about love and is working on love.* We've mentioned the kind of community we are trying to build in our own family. That isn't always possible; some families are scattered all over the world. But if you believe anything you have read in this book, please listen to this advice: *If you don't now belong to a community of people who are working on love, join one, or, if necessary, build one.*

I'm talking about a small community—like the apostles, like a family. A community small enough so that you can get to know one another, understand one another, and feel a part of one another.

I don't know what else to say as I close this book. I can't very well tell you, in a paragraph or two, how to discover or how to build a loving community. Jeanette and I have devoted our entire lives to this work. So have a lot of other people. Small prayer groups. The Christian Family Movement. Marriage Encounter. Keith Miller and his life's work. David and Vera Mace. A hundred others.

Still, all of these, as well as ourselves, are only searchers for that final way of building genuine, loving, caring communities. We are human beings who build communities as human beings build everything. We build the kinds that are right for us—and hope they are right for you.

Yet, all of us begin from one source. We all try to follow the same leader. We see Christ spending years of his precious and limited time in the intense, personal, and increasingly loving company of just 12 people. We study the community he built, as you can study it too. We try to understand the very human things that went on there, and are awed by the overwhelming results these ordinary people achieved.

You can have Christ for a guide, too. You can study him just as we did. You can talk with him just as the apostles did. He will lead you to a loving community that is right for you, if you sincerely ask him to, and if you are seriously committed to loving.

Loving someone and knowing that you are loved by someone—this is the greatest feeling in the world. It is a state of being that is worth any effort we put into it. It is what God wants for us. Love is the bread of life he offers each one of us.

But there is no free lunch at God's diner.